G. Gyfford

A Discourse Of The Subtill Practises Of Deuilles By Witches And Sorcerers

G. Gyfford

A Discourse Of The Subtill Practises Of Deuilles By Witches And Sorcerers

ISBN/EAN: 9783742839206

Manufactured in Europe, USA, Canada, Australia, Japa

Cover: Foto ©Andreas Hilbeck / pixelio.de

Manufactured and distributed by brebook publishing software
(www.brebook.com)

G. Gyfford

A Discourse Of The Subtill Practises Of Deuilles By Witches And Sorcerers

A
Discourse

of the subtill Practises

of Deuilles by Witches and
Sorcerers. By which men are
and haue bin greatly deluded: the
antiquitie of them: their diuers sorts and Names.

With an Aunswer vnto diuers friuolous Rea-
sons which some doe make to prooue that
the Deuils did not make those ope-
rations in any bodily shape.

By G. Gyfford.

Imprinted at London for
Toby Cooke. 1587.

A Discourse of the subtill Practises of Devills by Witches and Sorcerers. By which men are and have bin greatly deluded: the antiquitie of them: their divers sorts and Names. With an Aunswer unto divers frivolous Reasons which some doe make to proove that the Devils did not make those Aperations in any bodily shape. By G. Gyfford. Imprinted at London for Toby Cooke. 1587.

Dedication

To the right woorshipfull Maister Richard Martin, Alderman, and Warden of her Majesties Mint. THE sacred Scriptures (right worshipful) both of the olde and new Testament, do speake in sundrie places of Witches, Conjurers, and Sorcerers, and that such doings are in high detestation before God: but what these can do few of the vulgar sort do rightly understand. For the most part do ascribe unto them very foolishly, such power and efficacie in working, as in deede the devil is not able to perform, though God should enlarge his chaine and give him full scope, to doe all that he desireth. Againe, some few are of the minde that what soever is spoken in the holy Scriptures, or in other writers concerning things wrought by such kinds of people, it was not done by the devill, but was a mere craft and cozenage of the deceiptfull men and women, which have taken upon them such matters. That the holy scriptures have no meaning to teach that devils ever did any thing that way. And that all other writers have erred which maintaine the same power of devils. The opinion of these latter is grosse, and in some sort contumelious, being against the direct testimonies of Gods word. The vaine conceipt of those former, that is to say, of the multitude, which imagine that Witches can worke at their pleasure, and so are the common plague of the earth, breedeth so innumerable sins, that it is as a monster with many heads. It is no mervaile that ignoraunt men which despise the light of the gospel are deceived by the crafty illusions of Satan: but this may seeme strange, that men instructed in the truth should be abused and erre though not in the grossest maner, yet grosly: but in deed the things are sildome handled by the preachers of the holy word, at the least, in such full manner as might

cut downe all false opinions conceived in mens mindes about the same. I have therefore bin mooved uppon such consideration to take some travell, and set forth somewhat to convince mens vaine opinions therein. I had not this minde, to set forth any large discourse what hath bin Judged and deemed in former times by learned men, and what they testifie concerning the slights of devills by oracles, divinations and such vaine deceipt: but onely to give a taste to the simpler sort even from the doctrine of the bible unto which I do only leave. It may be some which have lofty mindes, whom nothing can content, but that which is to their thinking absolutely perfect, will say it is slender, and to no purpose. It is that which I am able, not written for those which knowe more, neather to seeke the cómendation of a learned worke: but in very deed to apply that small measure of knowledge which God in mercy hath given me, to the benefit of those that want it. If any with deeper skill shall reveale that which I have not attained unto, I will be right glad, not onely for my selfe, but also for our countrimen which greatly neede instruction in the same. I present it unto your worship, not for the greatnes of the worke, but to testifie my hearty good-will: which in respect of that loving favour, and friendship which your worship hath for certaine yeares shewed towards me, is great: but farre greater, because that your zeale hath bin shewed towards the gospell, and love towards al those that publish and professe it. I trust your worship will take in good part this poore gift, considering from what minde it cómeth: there bee some things handled in it, which are usually committed both in the city and in the country, that are horrible before God, and to be severely punished by such as are placed in authority, and therefore not unfit to be perused by them. The Lord which hath inriched your worship divers waies with his good gyfts, increase and double the same to his honor and your eternall comfort. Amen. Your worships to commaund. George Gyfford.

Body of Text

Page 4

A BRIEFE DISCOURSE wherein is declared the subtil practise of devils by witches and sorcerers, by which men are and have bene greatly seduced. The 1 Chapter I Am not ignorant touching this one point, that the discovery, and laying open of Satans wylines which hee practiseth by witchcraft, is a matter of no small difficulty, the reason is manifest, and without all controversie to bee admitted, which doth prove the same: for if politike wise men can dig so deepe to hide there counsels and intents, that no man can espie them: how shall wee discry the practice of devils, who are far more deepe and subtil, and can cover their sleights and false conveiances more craftily then men': let no man therefore suppose that I take upon me, or professe so great skil as to uncover and make manifest, as it were the groundwork of those treacheries which he practiseth by Sorcerers and Witches. The very truth is, I have not curiously serched them out, nether do I accompt it the labour best spent. I only purpose so far to open Satans packe, and to make shew of so many of his false and counterfeit wares, as may instruct the simple sort to discerne the better and to judge of all the rest, which I trust every modest and sober mynd will allow to bee in some measure sufficient. Seing we have this advantage, that wee are most sure that al his finest stuffe is no better then his coursest wares, because that all his doings are for naughty and wicked purpose, howsoever they may seeme to bee profitable, Whereas then the light of

Page 5

Gods word doth dispell the thicke darknes wherwith this slie enemie hydeth himselfe, and manifesteth his most pestiferous and deadly poison in some thinges, let it bee a sufficient warning for all his doinges, without further examination. I am moved to deale with this matter, (and I with it were dealt throughly in by such as are fully able) for this consideration, that I see many through ignorance of such things are greatly overreached by Satan, and so entangled and snared with errors that they fal into very foule and horrible sinnes: those that understand the Latine touge, may very wel satisfy themselves with that which wearines with great judgement and travell hath written touching this argument, I have not seene any that have written in our tong, which lead not into error on the one side or the other: for there be extremities on both sides into which men do fall. The most part have bene besotted, even such as did take themselves to be very wise: for they have berely believed that witches could do great monders, ascribing such power unto devils as belongeth onely to God. Others there bee which do stifly maintaine (but how wisely let it appeare) that all witchcraft spoken of, either in the holy Scriptures, or testifyed by other writers to have bene among the heathen, or in thee latter dayes, hath bene, and is no more but either more cosenage, or poisoning: so that in the opinion of these men, the devill hath never done, nor can do any thing by witches and sorceres. It may be some man will object, and say, what hart can grow from this opinion? Who can tell what hurt will ensue and grow thereof, unlesse he saw first some what by experience, this we all do see, that one carnell of wheat being sowen, doth grow up and bring forth a whole eare, with an hundredth carnels in it sometyme. If one error be planted, who can tell what increase it may yeeld in tyme': the grownd doth not bring forth the corne with such increase, as mans hart doth errors. If a man draw in one linke of a chaine, another followeth and is by and by in sight, which draweth wee know not how many after it, until we see the last. There is no error that goeth alone, or that is not linked unto other. The holy Scriptures

(which make the man of God perfect, and perfectly instructed unto every good worke) are for to judge and to decide all controversie in this case. I will therefore onely sticke unto them for testimonie and proofe. The definition of a witch: the antiquity of witchcraft. The 2 Chapter. THe perfect and right knowledge of thinges is, when a man doth know the causes. A definition both consist of those causes which give the whole essence and containe the perfect nature of the thing defined: therefore where that is found out, there is a very cleer light. If it be perfect, it is much the greater, though it be not fully perfect, yet it giveth some good light. For which respect though I dare out affirme, that I can give a perfect definition in this matter, which is hard to do even in knowen things, because the essential forme is hard to be found, yet I do give a definition, which may at the least give notice what manner of persons they be, of whom I mynde to speake. A Witch is one that worketh by the Devill, or by some develish or curious art, either hurting or healing, revealing things secrete, or foretelling thinges to come, which the devil hath devised to entangle and snare mens soules withal unto damnation. The conjurer, the enchaunter, the sorcerer, the diviner, and whatsoever other sort there is, are in deed compassed within this circle. The Devill after divers forces no doubt, and after divers formes doth deale in these, but who is able to shew an essential difference in each of them from all the rest': I hold it no wisedome, nor labour well spent to travell much therein, one artificer hath devised them al: they bee

Page 7

all to one ende and purpose, howsoever they may differ in outward rules for practice of them, that is litle or nothing besides mere delusion. Who wil not confesse that the father of lies is not to bee trusted': who knoweth not that all his doings are hidden under colourable sheives': shall men seeke for steadfastnes in his wayes': shall they be so folish as to Imagine, that things are effected by the vertue of wordes, gestures, figures, or such lyke': doubtless all those are but to deceive, and to draw men forward, and to plunge them more deeply into errors and sinnes. And now touching the antiquity of witchcraft, wee must needes confesse that it hath bene of very ancient tyme: because the holy Scriptures do plainly testify so much. For in the tyme of Moses it was very ryfe in Egypt. Neither was it newly sprong up: being common and growen unto such ripenes among the nations, that the Lord reckoning up divers kindes, saith that the gentils did commit such abominations, for which he would cast them out before the children of Israel, G1 Deutron. 18. How long it was before that tyme, can not for certainty be discussed: saving that (as we have said) it was not yong in those dayes, when Moses wrote. And if we maintaine that it was before the flood, ther is great reason to uphold and justify the affection. Wee know that the Devill was exceeding crafty from the beginning. Alwaies labouring to seduce and deceive after the woorst manner. If hee fayled of his desire, it was because men had not procured Gods displeasure to come upon them, to deliver them over unto strong delusion. G2 But we see how God complaineth, that men had wonderfully corrupted their wayes, long before the flood. God being G3 thus provoked by the wickednes of the world, what should make us doubt, but that through his just judgement, the devil had power given him, and was let lose, that hee might seduce and lead the profane Nations into the depth of the gulfe of all abominable sinnes, that they might have the sorer condemnation': -notes- G1 Deut. 18. G2 a Thes. 2. G3 Geu. 6.

Page 8

That there be 8.sortes of Witches and practisers of devilish art, mentioned, Deuter.18.whose names and their interpretation do here follow. The 3. Chapter. THer are no doubt a thousand waies differing every one from the rest in one circumstance or other, under which Satan doth hide and cover his craft and deadly poyson. But yet the holy Ghost to warne al men to beware, doth mention onely 8. sortes, under which no doubt hee comprehendeth all other: for there bee other names in the Scriptures, but yet such as do note in the Egyptian and Chaldeans tong, those that are the same with some of these. I suppose that this one reason may suffice for to prove, that under eight names all are comprehended, because that here is a general matter dealt in. For the Lord shewing that those gentils caused their children to passe through the fire doth by the trope synecdoche of the part for the whole, understand all that false worship and idolatrie into which they were blindly led and seduced. Then hee nameth who they were, whose helpe Satan did use as chiefe instrumentes to seduce withall. And lastly agaynst all these hee doth oppose the true Prophet, whom hee would raise up from tyme to tyme, unto his people, at whose mouth they were to learne his holy wil and the true and acceptable worship. Now then let us come unto the names by which those evill people are named by the holy ghost in the

Hebrew tong, for their interpretation, so farre as wee may attayne, wil bring some light hereunto. The most of them be set down in the forme of participles. The first is called Kosem Kesamim, that is, one which devineth by

divinations: the latter word is added for to distinguish, because the devining was more general then by divinations, as appeareth by that speech which Saul used unto the witch, when hee requested her to devine by her spirite, and to bring up him whom he should name. The word is sometime used in good part For in the third chapter of Esay, God doth threten for a plague that he will take away Kosem. And king Solomon Prou. 16. doth commend Kesem, that is divination in the lippes of the king, which should guide him in judgement. For in those places, Kosem is put for a man of excellent and rare giftes for government. In other places of the holy Scriptures, where it is taken in evill part, it is put for false prophets which with G1 their lying and vaine divinations did seduce the people. G2 These did sometyme devise lies: sometyme they did dreame dreams, which they followed and propounded to the people, as if they had receaved them from God, for God did use that as one way to reveale himselfe to his servants, when as in deed they were in these diviners but the vanities of their owne hartes, and illusions of unclean spirites which alwaies counterfait the holy spirite of God. Sometyme the devill did inspire them, and shew them visions, as if he had bene the holy Ghost, and made them utter his wares under the name of God. This matter is sufficiently proved by the history which is written 1 Reg. 22 for there it is shewed, that to the end king Ahab might bee seduced and goe up to Ramoth Gyliad unto battaile, a devill hath power given him to be a lying spirite in the mouth of the 400 false prophets which were Ahabs. Divers thinges are in that place set forth to the reach of our capacity, but this is clere what effect it wrought, for both the Prophets and Ahab were deceived. Sometyme the Lord himselfe did speake unto Kosem, though we never read that any true Prophet was so called but sorcerers, which did fetch answers and divinations from the devil, whom they tooke to be God, hee did so cunningly handle the matter. But wee do not reade in the holy Scripture of any more but one sorcerer, whom the Lord spake unto. And that was Balaam, for he is called Kosem Jos, 13.ver.22 -notes- G1 Jech 22. G2 Mich. 3.

which name sheweth that hee was no Prophet of the Lord, hee was accustomed to fetch answers from the Devill, why els did hee will those that were sent from the King to stay all night, to see what answere hee should have: It is sayd afterward, that he went Likkath Kesamim, that is, to meet with divinations. A thing which hee was accustomed unto: but at this tyme God himselfe did speake unto him. The second is called Megnonen, from whence this name was derived, none can for certainty affirme, for it may come Gnun, whereof commeth Gnonah, which signifyeth a set tyme for any purpose. It may also as well bee derived from Gnanan, which is a clowd. If whether of them it commeth, it is usually taken for such as did practise Indiciarie Astrologie, which from the course of the heavens, and the stars, did take upon them to foreshew warres, pestilences, seductions, treasons, and the death of great Princes. Moreover they did teach the fit and prosperous times for to buy or to sel: to journey by Sea or by Lande, to make peace, to undertake warre, or to marry. These also did take upon them to shew unto ever man (so that they did know the instant of his byrth) whether he were borne under a lucky or an unlucky planet. What vertue or what vice he should be given unto: whether he should be rich or poore, learned, or unlearned, what manner of death hee should dye. Agaynst these God did invey by his Prophets, declaring their vanity, accompting them among the witches and sorcerers. Their errors are very vyle and abhominable by which they did seduce the blynd. Wee may see how the Lord doth speake of them Jesay chapter 47. ver.13. where hee calleth them Hobereschammaim, that is, observers of the Heavens, and Chozim baccahochabim, gazers uppon the Starres. It is not the mynde of the Lord to condemne the observing and beholding of the course of the Heavens, and the Starres: for G1 they set foorth the great glory of the Creator, as these are much to blame, which do not diligently behold them, to be stirred up unto admiration and worshiping of the great God. G2 But -notes- G1 Psalm 8. G2 Psalm 19.

Page 11

those Astrologians did behold them awisse, ascribing all good thinges unto them, which are peculier unto God, likewise the evil thinges which are from the devil, and from the corrupted nature of man by original sinne. Yea they tye the providence of God unto the Starres. For if there bee any sound vertue in a man, it is of grace through fayth, and not from the Starres, drotkennes, adultery, murther, disobedience, cruelty, and such like are of the Devill, and from the nature of man by him corrupted in the fall of Adam. If a man should aske these vaylie fooles whether the nature of the starres bee changed since mans fall, what will they answere: for this they must needes confesse, that if the Starres bee the cause and fountaine of vice in men, then they bee either changed from their first creation from good into evill, or else that God created the cause and fountayne of evill. And so as they committe vile sacrilege on the one side, when they make the starers the bestowers of vertues, lykewise on the other side they fall into horrible blasphemie when they make God the creator of the cause of evil. The holy Scriptures do teach, that vice and uncleannes is in us from our sinfull parentes, and that the Devill brought it in and doth increase the same: famins, pestilences, and cruell warres are sent by the wrath of God for sinne. The wise Astrologians tell us of this and that conjunction of planets, which wil cause tyrants to rage, frendes to be false one to an other, women will bee disobedient to their husbandes: these thinges in deed come much to passe, and folish people believe that the Astrologians did foresee it by the Starres. If men did prosper, it was ascribed unto that lucky planet under which they were borne. In adversity they blamed the Starres, warres, pestilences, and famins being thought in come from them, men never consider their sinnes which have bene the cause of Gods indignation (for those thinges hee sendeth as the roddes and scourges of his wrath) but are led into a further mischiefe: for now they fall to worship the host of Heaven. And as the Lord saith, Jerem 10. They feare the signes of Heaven. For this is mans nature, that where hee is

Page 12

perswaded that there is the power to bring prosperity and adversity, there will hee worship. In respect therefore of this, the Astrologians are litle better then witches. For the devill doth seduce by them. Some will exclaime that wee do now condemn the excellent and noble skill of Astronemie. But that is nothing so. For it is a precious gift which God hath given unto men, wherby they are able to take view of his works which are so high above them. Men do behold goodly things so sone as they cast their eies upon the heavens. But such as have the skill of Astronomie doe behold a great deal more. All men do see a glorious trimme worke, but yet a far off. Whereas the Astronomers are after a sort carried up hard to it, and see those things which common sense doth not attaine. It is verifyed uppon all which the Prophet sayth: the heavens declare the glory of God. For what minde is so blunt, but doth conceive that the divine power is great, and glorious, which made, set in order, and susreineth such a worke: The rudest sort do find that the course of the Sunne and the Mone do order the dayes, and the nightes, moneths, and yeares, Winter and Sommer: Who perceiveth not what great power the Sunne hath with his cherishing heate to cause thinges to grow: the Mone beareth a great sway in the waters. Divers other thinges there be which are manifest to the simple. But how farre beyond al these goethe learned Astronomers, which do come nigh to gather the distance, and withall the wonderfull greatnes of the celestiall bodies, and their incomprehensible swiftnesse: incomprehensible I say unto man. When from these they turne their eyes towardes the Creator. How can they but bee amazed at the consideration of his greatness: they see the severall courses of planets, and their motions, and the same fixed by an unchangeable decree: how can they cease wondering at the wisedom of God, who hath so skilfully fashioned them with that which is secrete unto others, as the influences and powers, is apparant in some measure unto them. Hens death either for the time or for the manner is not subject to the stares: much less vertue or vice are

Page 13

ingendred in mens myndes by them. The Astronomers do very grosly erre in these predictions about windes and showers: but yet no doubt there bee many thinges which depend much upon the course of the heavens: which is no derogation to the providence of God, who hath ordayned, and doth use them as instruments for the same. Great operations in the bodies of men and beasts, as all skilful phisitions do find, come from the planets. And no doubt the devil tooke occasion hereby for to lead men further in these thinges then they should have gone. The third is called Menachesh. Nachash signifyeth to conjecture, from whence the same is derived. Laban when he intreated Jacob to abide still with him, doth use that woord. I have (saith he) conjectured, or found by experiments that God G1 hath blessed me for thy sake. For hee felt that his cattle did increase and thrive under his hand. Joseph when hee had caused his silver cup to be put into the sacke of his brother Benjamin, and upon search being found in the same, speaketh after the same maner: and sayth he did devine or conjecture by that cup what manner of men they were. It seemeth that the word was used indifferently, and often times taken in good part. When it is taken in evill part, it semeth to note such as in Latine are called Augures: A kind of soothsayiers, which did conjecture and prophesie by the voices, and by the flying of Birdes by the intrals of beasts, and other like observations. These were common among the heathe, and had in great estimation. For the wiser sort did beleeve that the Gods (as they use to say) did use the tonges of birdes as theire interpreters, to make thinges knowen unto men. The like for the flying of birds, which they did observe when they went about any matter. Hereupon some were accompted luckie and some unlucky birds. And how the devil did play to deliver men by the intrals of beasts, who knoweth? the thing is not now in practise: but yet some reliques and dregs of this kind of witchcraft (if I may so cal it) do remaine among us. For some will gather by the chattering of pyes, that they shal have gestes come unto them. The raven he sitteth upon the steeple and cryeth:which way doth he looke sayth one, -notes- G1 Gen. 30.

from thence ye shal have an eie ere it be long. Another goeth abrode early in the morning, and a hare crosseth his way: a very unlucky signe he taketh it to be, and looketh not to speede well that day. Frends meet together and make mery: some one at unwares doth turn down the salt: the man or the woman towards whom it falleth, doth blush and take little comfort of the dainty banquet. For that is taken to be a grievous evil sign of mishap that will follow. Heavy newes is brought unto some, that her father, or her mother, or her brother is dead: I did even looke for such a matter (saith the) for my nose this day did sodainly break forth a bleeding. Thus hath the devill crept into the mindes of unbeleeving people, and causeth them to turne their eies from God. These things must we condemne, but we must take heed that we do not withal disallow those things which are to be approved. For no doubt, as we see by experience, fowls and beasts do foreshew some things, but yet by a natural cause. The goose and the ducke, and divers other water fowles, do dive and wash them and make a great sturre against raine. The crow he cryeth otherwise then ordinary. Other fowls there be, which do flocke together and come up from the sea, when a cold blast is toward. The cow, though shee bee not very nimble, nor taketh great pride in her running, yet setteth up her taile, and about shee goeth the fields. The litle gnat soundeth her trumpet and giveth warning of a shower. What shall wee say to these and a number such like? that they be as the heathen said the interpreters of the gods: no verely, but there is a natural cause, and that is this: the disposition of the ayre is changed, and that do these fowles and beasts feel in their bodies, which maketh them so to deale, that ther is such a change in the disposition of the aire, though common sense in men, do not perceive it, yet many things do shew. What maketh the salt to bee wet, but that the moysture of the ayre doth dissolve it': what what maketh the marble stone to sweat against raine, but even the moisture of the aire which it draweth to it': what maketh the soot to fal downe by lumps and gobs out of the chimney, but the moist ayre against rayne doth loosen it': If any man wil yet doubt how the fowls or beasts should feele

the change of the ayre in their bodies: hee may see it is not a thing strange. For a man whose arme or his leg hath bene broken, or that hath had some mayme or sore bruse in his bodye, doth feel a great ache against rayne: this doth come of the alteration of the air. And thus wee see it behoveth men to discerne betweene such things as have a natural cause, and therby do after a sort foreshew things: and those which have no cause in nature, but are to be rejected. The 4 is called. Mechashshepha. It is derived from Cashaph, which is found in the holy scriptures, and that is 2 cron. 33. 6. what the word doth properly signify, or from whence it is drawen, can no man tel. More then this, that it is used for a kind of witches and sorcerers. Some do imagine that it was such a one as did deale, not by the devil, but by poison only, so that in their opinion, where it is translated, thou shalt not suffer a witch to live Ex. 22. It should be more fitly said, thou shalt not suffer a prisoner to live. But this is of ignorance, for the matter is far otherwise, as shall be shewed: their opinion is grounded upon the greeke translation, which is asscribed unto the 70 interpreters: for they do translate this word Mechashshepha Pharmacous, which say they do signify such as did make and use poison. The first error is iu this, that they consider not that Pharmacha are as wel good confections and holsom medicines, as poisons: this is manifest that witches do take upon them to deale with medicines and confections which they use together with their charmes: they make divers ointmentes, which Satan doth use to delude them withall. He teacheth them also to make poisons: wherupon this is cleere that the greeke woord Pharmakeia is used as a generall name for witchcraft and sorcery, as we may se in divers places of the new testament. S. Paul. Gal. 5. reciting the works of the flesh useth that word for witchcraft. Babilon is charged that she had seduced the nations by her witchcraft: wheras in deed that word is used. But if any man shall say these profes are weake, and do not make the matter so clere as to be out of all controversie, then let them consider a second error in those which hold opinion, that Mechashshepha, was one which dealt only with

poison, and not by the devil: for howsoever the signification of the word can not be found, yet we find plainly expressed in the scriptures what this kind of witch did. In the 2 chap. of Dan. Nabuchadnezer among others whom hee would have to interprete his neame, sendeth also for Mechashshephim. If these were poisoners what should they do about such a busines': we see that among the Chaldeans, and even in the kings court, they were had in great estimation, as wise men, and interpreters of secrets. If either the name it selfe had signifyed, or their practise shewed them to be poisoners, how could they have bin esteemed': Is any man so absurd as to thinke that kinges would take poisoners for their chief wise men? Moses doth report that when Aaron had cast downe his staffe before the K. of Egypt, and it was turned into a serpent, he sent for his wise men, and his enchaunters and they did the like, For every man cast downe his staffe before Pharaoh, and they were turned into serpents. These enchaunters which made the appearance of serpentes, and of frogges, and of turning water into blood, are first in that place called Mechashshephim, and then Chartummim: what shall wee say then, that the king of Egypt called for poisoners, and that they were indeede but poisoners that wrought such feats before him? I suppose this is plaine enough unto al that will not wilfully bend themselves to cavill, for to prove that Mechashshepha is not a poisoner, but a witch. This kinde is that which I mynd chiefly to speake off, with some that follow and therefore in this place I do omit to speake further. The 5 is called Chober chabar, which is one that doth enchaunt by enchauntment. Chabar doth signify to associate and joyne together: this enchaunter as it seemeth is so called of the society which he hath with the devil. Lachath semeth to be the same: for they are put both for one Psal. 58. And this latter word doth signify to whisper. For Chober had his charme of words and sentences, which he did whisper: they tooke uppon the to do many things by their charms: but the holy scriptures do mention but one. And that is of snakes and serpentes which they did charm. From hence the prophet David fetcheth a coparison

Page 17

Psal. 58. by which he sheweth that ther is no good counsel, though it be given by most excellent men, which can recover the wicked fró their ungodlines. But they stop their eares against it, or it doth not sincke into them: this his comparison is in these words, pethen which he useth is not the adder, but the basilisks or some kind of exceding venimous serpent which stoppeth his eares, and wil not heare the voice of the charmer G1 though he were a most skilful enchanter. Solomon giving instruction how a man is to appease the wrath of the ruler, doth bring a comparison also fró hence to admonish a man that hath wisedome to use it so in this matter, of asswaging the anger of the prince, that it come not to late. Thus he speaketh, if ý serpet bite where ther is no charm, what profit is there to him that is lord of ye tong': he calleth there the lord or master of ye tong, not as it is cómonly taken, a babler, but he that had skil to use his tong by charms as enchautments: which came to late and could stand him in no stead after the serpent had stong him, and so the wisdom which is in a man may come to late. The Schoel ob, which is as much as to say, one which enquireth, as Ob, sometyme bagnalath Ob, one that possesseth Ob. And somtyme it G2 is sayd, the man or the woman in whom there is Ob, as Liuit. 20 Ob is used for a bottle, or some hollow vessel. But by these places which I have cited it is manifest that the witch and Ob are distinguished: for ye witch is not called Ob, but enquireth at Ob: and is sayd to possesse Ob: wherby wee may see that the devil was called Ob: for what cause I know not, but it is supposed, because hee did speak with a hollow voice, as it were out G3 of a tub or a bottle. I, els as it is sayd, Thy voice shall bee like Ob out of the ground: this same kind is thought of the most learned to be that devil which the Grecians called Pythe. S. Luke doth report Act. 16. that at Philippos there was a mayd which had a devil in her whom he calleth a spirite of Pytho: and this maid did deuine, and brought great gayne to her maysters thereby. The oracles of the heathen in old time, were fró such. And of this we are also to speake more afterward, but I take it a thing very manifest, that if Pytho were only a devil which -notes- G1 Eccl. 10. G2 1 Sam. 28 G3 Esay. 29.

Page 18

spake out of a mayde, as this in the Acts, and the Sygnillæ were maids, for the devil which fayned himselfe to bee a great God, seemed ye it must be a virgin preest out of who he must speake, then Ob was more general. For he did not alwayes speak out of the witch, nether did they alwayes demand to know ye matter of him, but he was sent to fetch up the soule of him, whom ye party would speake withal, as appeareth by the words of Saul For he biddeth her devine by Ob, and fetch up him who he should name. The 7. is named Jiddegnoni. Jadang is to know from whece this word semeth to be derived. For such as deale with devils do know many things, which other men can not know so far as God doth permit unto the devil to reveale: this kind is commonly joyned with Shoel Ob, and therefore thought to differ litle from the same. For they both wrought with the Devill as doe the Witches, and also the Conjurers. Either of them no doubt may verie wel set forth both our Witches and Conjurers, though there seem to be great difference between them, which is no more in deed, but the craft of the devil. His auncient manner of practise with Shoelob and Jiddegnoni have bene detected, and therefore he hath turned thinges into an other forme, but the matter are the same. Conjurer goeth one way to work, and the witch an other, the one as it seemeth for on purpose, the other for an other, but yet the chiefe end is all one. The eyght and last is called Doresh el hammethim, that is as much as to say, on which enquireth at the dead. This kind of witch was called of the grecians Necromantes, that is one which useth divinations by the dead. And the art it self was called Necromancia. I see not how this could much differ fró Bagnalath Ob, which tooke upon her to fetch up the soules of dead men. These were so called not that they were able by any meanes to featch up the soule of any man either good or bad. But the devill feined him selfe to be the soule of such or such a body, and handled the matter so that they could perceive none other. Thus much may suffice for the names used in the holy scriptures. There be other, but no doubt the same indeed with some of these. How to proceed for ward, and to shew what any

of these did or could doe by sorceries, it is requisite in the first place to speak of the cheife doer, which is the devill. The nature of devils described with there operations and effects. The 4 Chapter. The Devils being the principall agents, and chiefe practisers in witchcrafts and sorceryes, It is much to the purpose to descrybe and set the for whereby we shall bee the better instructed to see what he is able to do, in what maner, and to what ende and purpose, At ye beginning (as Gods word G1 doth teach us) they were created holy Angels, full of power, and glory. G2 They sinned, they were cast downe from heaven, they were utterly deprived of glory, and preserved for judgement. This therfore, and this change of theirs, did not destroy nor take away their former faculties: but utterly corrupt, pervert, and deprave the same: the essence of spirits remayned, and not onely but also power and understanding, such as is in Angels, ye heavely Angels are very mighty and strong, far above all earthly creatures in the whole world. The infernall angels are for their strength called principalityes and powers those blessed ones applye G3 all their might to set up and advaunce the glory of God, to defend and succor his children, the devils bend all their force against G4 God, agaynst his glory, his truth and his people. G5 And this is done with such fiercenes, rage, and cruelty, that the holy ghost G6 paynteth them out under the figure of a great red or fiery dragon, and roaring lyon, in very deed any thing comparable to the: G7 He hath such power and authority indeede, that hee is called the God of the world. His kingdome is bound and inclosed within certayne limits, for he is ý prince but of darknes: but yet within his sayd dominion (which is in ignorance of God, he exerciseth a mighty tyrany, our Savior compareth him to a strong man armed which kepeth his castle. -notes- G1 2Pct.2. G2 Jude. G3 Ephes. G4 Psalm. 34. G5 Heb. 1. G6 Revel. 21. G7 1. Pet. 5.

And what shall we saie for the wisedome and understanding of Angels, which was given them in their creatió, was it not far above that which men can reach unto? When they became divels (even those reprobate angels) their understanding was not taken awaie, but turned into malicious craft and subtiltie. He never doth any thing but of an evill purpose, and yet he can set such a colour, that the Apostle saith he both change himselfe into the likenesse of an angell of light. For the same cause he is called the old serpent, he was subtill at the beginning, but he is now growne much more subtill by long experience, and continuall practise, he hath searched out and knoweth all the waies that may be to deceive. So that if God should not chaine him up, as it is set forth Revel. 20. his power and subtiltie joyned together, would overcome and seduce the whole world. There be great multitudes of infernall spirits, as the holy scriptures doe everie where shew, but yet they doe so joine together in one, that they be called the divell in the singular number. They doe all joine together (as out saviour teacheth) to uphold one kingdome. G1 For though they can not love one another indeede, yet the hatred they beare against God, is as a band that doth tye them together. The holie angels are ministering spirits, sent foorth for their sakes which shall inherit the promise. They have no bodilie shape of themselves: but to set foorth their speediness, the scripture applieth it selfe unto our rude capacitie, and painteth them out with wings. When they are to rescue and succour the servants of God, they can straight waie from the high heavens, which are thousands of thousands of miles distant from the earth, bee present with them. Such quickness is also in the divels: for their nature being spirituall, and not loden with any heavie matter as our bodies are, doth affoord unto them such a nimblnes as we can not conceive. By this they flie through the world over sea and land, and espie out al advantages and occasions to doe evill. -notes- G1 Mat. 12.

Now to declare what these malignant wicked divels have effected and brought to passe, or what great successe they have attained, would be a long and tedious piece of worke. A G1 few short sentences of the word of God onely to note the same, may suffise in this behalfe: he prevailed by his great G2 craft against our first parents: he is called the prince of this world, and the God of this world. The Gentiles did worship G3 divels, since the comming of our Saviour Christ, when hee was bound for a thousand yeares, being let loose againe, hee G4 seduced the world: yea he was the means, and it was by the G5 efficacie of his power, that Antichrist the Pope and his false religion was set up. And so all the world wondered and followed the beast (for so the holy ghost termeth Antichrist) and G6 they worshipped the beast, and they worshipped the dragon which gave power to the beast. This seemeth horrible and monstrous, that all nations of the world should worship the divell: doubtless they never meant it, but when they forsooke the true worship prescribed in the holie word, and imbraced idolatrie, and woorship devised by man, whatsoever intent they had, God laieth to their charge that they woorshipped divels. What victories the divell hath gotten at other times in the world, doth sufficiently appeare by this, that he is described with seven G7 crownes. He hath raised up all kinds of heretiks, he hath stirred up fore persecutions against the Church, and caused the servants of God to be cruellie murthered. Thus much touching Divels. -notes- G1 Gen. 3. G2 2. Cor. 4. G3 2. Cor. 10. G4 Revel. 20. G5 2. These. 2. G6 Revel. 13. G7 Revel. 12.

Page 22

Devils have no power to hurt mens bodies or goods, but upon speciall leave given unto them. The 5. Chapter. The reprobat angels are mightie, fierce and subtill, as we have brieflie noted. They be instrumentes of Gods vengance, and executioners of his wrath, they doe not exercise power and authoritrie which is absolute, and at their owne will and appointment, but so farre as God letteth foorth the chaine to give them scope. Touching the reprobat, which despise the waies of God and are disobedient, we are taught, that God in righteous vengeance giveth thé over into their hands, for they would not love his lawes, nor honour him as their God: therefore they come under the tirannie of wicked G1 divels, which worke in them with power, their harts do they harden, their eies, even the eies of their minds do they blind, they kindle and stir up in them all filthie lusts, and carrie them headlong into foule and abhominable sinnes. Here is their throne and kingdome, not that they be able to carrie these so far as they would, but as every one doth more grievously provoke God, so are they plunged y deeper, either into monstrous heresies, or abhominable wickednesse, for God giveth them over into a reprobat mind, some indeed are caried further thá other into the depth of impietie, because G2 God letteth him more stronglie invade them, and taketh away his graces and gifts, but yet he raigneth in them all, in as much as they be void of the power of grace to resist him, and are caried captives by him unto eternall damnation. These wicked fiends doe also set upon the faithfull and G3 elect people of God, for God useth them also as instruments for their triall, they tempt and trie them, they doe wrestle G4 and fight against them, they buffet them, every way seeking to annoy and molest them both in bodie and soule. God indeed turneth all unto the good of these. Hee letteth him - notes- G1 Ephes.2. G2 Rom.1. G3 Ephes.6. G4 2.Cor.12.

Page 23

have power and scope no further upon them, than he giveth strength and power of grace to resist, at the least so farre that the wicked one can not cause them to sinne unto death. This G1 then being out of al controversie, that his power even in that wherein it is greatest, and where he seemeth to have his chiefe right, is limited: how shall it be deemed but that touching the bodies of both men and beasts, or of anie other creature, be can doe nothing but upon speciall leave and commission graunted unto him. He can not doe violence to the bodie of a poor swine, naie he can not at his pleasure kill so much as a seelie flie. When God will have him to touch anie creature, either man, beast, fish, foul, tree, corne, or whatsoever, he flieth upon it, and maketh the greatest shew that he can. These things are we plainlie taught in the holie scriptures, not onelie by those which were possessed with divels, and were greevouslie tormented in bodie: but also by destroying both men and cattle. In the booke of Job the first chapter, we are plainely taught, first that the divell could not touch Job, nor any thing that was his, then that having leave, he slew his children, destroied his servants and cattell, and plagued him in his bodie with sores, the holie ghost doth so manifestlie teach that the divell did this, that to denie it is flac impietie, and the vaine and frivolous cavils to proove the contrarie not woorth the answering. The holie ghost doth applie himself in that place to our rude capacitie. It is very true: and so doth he in manie places of the holy scriptures, doth it follow therefore that the things were not: We are not capable of things spirituall, and therefore they be set forth under the forme of things corporal and visible. We may not imagine that devils thrust in themselves amongst the holie angels into the glorious presence of God in Heaven. Neither must we suppose that GOD talketh with the divell and he with him: but these and such like things are borrowed to set before us things invisible. God useth the divels by his providence to accomplish the -notes- G1 John.5.

woorke which he determineth, eyther in wrath upon the wicked,
or for chastisement and tryall of his Children. What could more
fitly expresse the same, then to liken him to a king which hath
servants and officers for every purpose, who came before him to
give an account what they have done, and to receive
commaundement what they shall doe: God limiteth their
baundes, he restraineth, he enlargeth them at his good pleasure.
But how Satan doth knowe where leave is given him, we cannot
conceive. For as it is sayd, God tolde him, all that he hath is in
thy hand: for us hee is brought in speaking in this wise, thou
hast hedged about him, and about all that he hath. Yea but Job
saith, God did all: And Job saith very true, but Job did knowe
God did it by appointing the Divell to doe it. He knew that the
theeves and murtherers which slewe his servaunts and drove
away his cattell, were stirred up by the Devill, he stayeth not
aboute them nor yet about the Devill, but looketh and
addresseth himselfe unto him which hath rule over men and
Devils, shall we say then God did it, therefore the Devill did it
not: It may be objected, that if the Devill did those thinges, then
is hee able to raise up mighty windes, tempests, lightning and
thunders. If hee sent that mighty winde, which did throwe downe
the house upon Jobs Children: If he cast downe that fire upon
the Cattell and Servauntes. Why may not men thinke that upon
leave he can do the other? I answere, that the scripture
ascribeth the Windes, the Tempests, the Waile and the mighty
Thunders and Lightnings unto God even as works peculier to his
Majestie, by which be doth set forth his magnificence and glory.
Because he alone hath created them, the devils are not able to
create any thing, though never so small, much lesse those
greate thinges. He seeth right well the matter whereof they
consiste and how they are by the naturall course which God bath
set, brought foorth, upon leave graunted unto him, he is able in
some sorte to collect the matter of them, or being prepared by
the Lord, to make them more violent: he doth covet also in the
darkest tempests, in the moste

raging windes, and terrible crackes of thunder to convey himselfe
into the storme, to come with it, and to shew some terrour of his
presence. For if it be graunted, he appeareth unto some in an
uglye shape, or renteth up trees. And this he doth to bring men
in beliefe that all those terrible thinges wherein there is so
glorious and so mighty power shewed, are his workes. And
herein he hath greatly bewitched the blind world, for it is a

common opinion, when there are any mighty windes and thunders with terrible lightnings, that the Devills is abroad and doth it. When they heare of houses burnt, or trees rent up and other harms by Sea or by Lande, by and by they begin to suspect that there have beene conjurors abroad, then rumors are spread, the conjurors, sayth one, are taken, they have confessed that they raised up Devils, and that three are broken loose, yea five, saith another, and how they wil get them in againe God knoweth, this wicked folly which possesseth the mindes of the ignorant sort, is a fruit of Poperie, For they tooke away the light, and the Devill did delude them in the darke at his pleasure, for beholde the wisedome of their greate Prelates in this poynt. Had they not hallowed belles to ring in greate tempestes, that the Devill might be driven awaie, as not able to come within the sounde of them: Did not these grave fathers beleeve that those great and terrible thinges were wrought by the Devill: And the greater they were, the rather men ascribed them unto Devils, a vile and brutish impietie, that the more glory did appeare, the sooner they shoulde attribute the same unto the Divill, but in very deed it is the G1 glorious GOD which causeth it to thunder, but it may be thought for all this, that the Devill doth bring lightning and thunder, and mightie windes, because as it seemeth those were no lesse which be did for to plague Job. I will shewe therefore that there is greate difference betweene the mighty workes of God, and those which are asscribed there, unto the Devill, they indeed seeme to be as great lightning, and thundering, as strong windes, but yet -notes- G1 Psal. 29.

Page 26

they are not, the Devil causeth fire to fall downe uppon the servauntes and the cattell of Job and burneth them. Let us see whether that bee like unto the lightning and thunder, God createth them and sendeth them in the Cloudes with mighty power and terror, they passe through the earth and upon the seas at his commaundement, the Devils did not make nor create that fire, but being already scattered in the ayre a company of them doe gather it together and cast it uppon the men and the beasts and make it [illegible word] upon them, this may seeme a very great matter above that which it is, unlesse we consider how it was done. First this is evident that the sun in the beames therof, being the fountaine of heate, there is fire dispersed: because when they be collected or the scattered heate which is in them, drawe together, they do burne, as experiece doth teach by some glasses which being holden in ye sun, Plutarch sheweth concerning the holy fire which the virgines called vestals, did keepe, ordeyned by Numa, that when it was out, either by negligence or mishap, it might not be kindled from common fire: but they had a way to collect the beames of the sun. We see also that by striking a sharpe flint and a sharpe Iron together, there commeth very burning fire. It doth not come out of the stone, nor yet out of the Iron, for so much fire as with a multitude of strokes is brought out of a little stone and a small Iron, could not bee in them, but they must needs be very hot, whereas indeed they be very cold, thus therefore it is: God hath so ordeined that in this whole worlde there cannot be Vacuum, that is to say, any place void or emptye, but it must needs be filled with sowhat, there is no power in man to make such empty place, so much as a pins head: for somewhat must fill the roome, we see therfore that water will not run out at the bottom of a vessel that hath holes, unlesse there be way for the ayre to come in, to fill the roome, put a bottle into the water being empty, you shall well perceave that it is ful of ayre, for no water wil into it but as the ayre goeth out, even so when a man striketh a sharpe stone, upon the sharpe edge of Steele, bee parteth the Ayre in

sunder at some strokes, that if there were not a quicker thing then ayre, there would for some moment of time be Vacuum, the fire therfore being dispersed doth gather to a sparke and fill the place where the ayre was parted. What marvel is it the though a sorte of malignant spirites, which have farre greater power and skill then men, do collect the fire which is scattered in the ayre, and drawe it downe upon men. This is nothing to the terrible lighteninges and thunders, which the mighty God hath created and ordereth. But what for the boisterous windes, did not Sathan raise as greate as is seemeth as the greatest when it threw downe the house, which no doubt was strong, for Jobs Children were no beggers. A answere that this winde was even the Devill or a company of Devils which moved the ayre and came rushing upon the house themselves with noyse, and threw it downe. It doth follow heereof that the Devill can send foorth windes as the Lord doth, which at his commaundement goe foorth over the large kingdomes of the earth, and over the wide Seaes, this is a worke farre above the power of Devils, and therefore the Divel hath bewitched those which beleeve that hee can doe such thinges. The Divels have power also to infect the humors in mens bodies, and of beasts likewise to bring sores and diseases, when God giveth him leave, this might suffice to proove that the Divels have no power to hurte, but uppon graunted, and that the same obteyned, they can do much, but yet I will adde one testimonie, because it is very cleare, and bringeth the matter out of all doubt, leaving no place for any cavill, the Evangelists doe report that our Saviour did cast Divels out of a man possessed. They besought him that they might enter into a great heard of swine which was feeding in the mountaines, he gave them leave, and the whole heards was carryed into the Sea and drowned in the waters. We see they could not touch the Swine without leave, and when that was granted, what mischiefe they wrought, thus much for this poynt.

Page 28

Divels can appeare in a bodily shape, and use speeche and conference with men. The 6. Chapter. Our Saviour Christ saith that a spirite hath neither flesh nor bones. G1 A spirite hath a substance, but yet such as is invisible, whereupon it must needes be graunted, that Divels in their owne nature have no bodilye shape, nor visible forme, moreover it is against the truth, and against pietie to beleeve, that Divels can create or make bodies, or change one body into another for those things are proper to God. It followeth therfore that whensoever they appeare in a visible forme, it is no more but an apparition and counterfeit shewe of a bodie, unlesse a body be at any time lent them. And when as they make one body to beare the likenes of another, it is but a colour. But some man wil say, what reason is there to shew that they can doe so much, being of an essence invisible: We may not staye heere within they limites of our owne reason, which is not able to reach onto, or to comprehend what way Devils should be able to have such operations. We may not I say measure their nimblenes, and power, and subtilties in working, by our owne understanding or capacitie. But we must looke what the holy scripture doth testifie in this behalfe, and therin rest and stay our selves. We have a manifest proofe, Exod.7.that the Devill can take a bodily shape. For when Aaron had cast downe his staffe and it was turned into a Serpent, the Enchaunters of Egypt cast downe their staves and they became Serpents, which was indeede, but in shew and appearance which the Devil made, for he deluded the senses, both in hiding the forme of the staves which indeede were not any -notes- G1 Luke. 24.

Page 29

way changed: and also in making a shewe of such bodies as were not, this was done openly and in ye cleare light, for otherwise it might be thought to be a meere illusion. For we see that men in extreme sickenes thinke they heare a voyce and see a shape, which none other in presence eyther heareth or seeth, some are so melancholike that they imagin they heare and see that which they doe not, for Sathan deludeth the phantasie so sore, that the partye doth suppose that his very outward senses do perceave the matter, but here was no such thing: but all which were with Pharao thinke there be very Serpents indeede, saying that Moses and Aaron did knowe it was the jugling of the Devill. Sing Saule when God had G1 forsaken him, and being in distresse sought unto a Witch. He is desirous to talke with Samuell which was dead, for he annointed him to be king over Israell. He requesteth of the witch that she would bring him up, she taketh the matter upon her, there commeth up one which taketh upon him to be Samuell, and the Scripture calleth him so, Saul and the witch take it to be so. He appeareth in a bodily shape, and useth goodly plaine speeche. It was not the true, but a false and counterfeit Samuel, even a wicked Devill, For be handleth the matter very cunningly, but yet in divers things bewrayeth himselfe. He was content that Saull should fall downe and worship him, which the true Samuell would never have suffered. He doth not rebuke him for seeking unto a witch, which the scripture condemneth. And the Lord imputeth it unto Saull G2 for one of the sinnes for which he did destroy him. In which place the Lord saith he sought to consult with Ob. This is out of doubt that the holy Ghost is far from calling the soul of Samuel Ob. and as for the woman she is not called Ob, but Bagnalath Ob, on which possesseth Ob. Nowe let us consider his speech, why, saith he, hast thou disquieted me, by calling me up: Marke what subtilty there is in these fewe wordes. This is most certaine, that the soules of righteous men are not subject to the call of a witch, but the crafty Devil would make men believe that they be, and even drawen foorth and -notes- G1 1. Sam. 28. G2 2. Cro. 10.

Page 30

troubled, or disquieted. For his speech is Lammab Hirgazinant, which is as much as to say, wherefore hast thou caused me to shake or be disquieted with feare: It is derived of Ragaz which is to shake and tremble. Would the true Samuell make men believe that the witch with her Ob. had such power to fetch him up: If it were Samuel indeed, why did he not rather say that God sent him: Againe the common error was that the soules of the righteous were in some place beneath in the earth where the witches familier spirite could come, and bring them up, and for this cause also this counterfeite Samuell saith he had made him come up. Abrahams bosome was Paradise, and S. Paule was taken up into the thirde G1 heaven and that he saith was Paradise. Then Samuell must have come downe, and not have come up. We see then that his speeche tendeth to confirme wicked and abhominable errors, which may suffice to proove that it was a Devill. Furthermore Moses doth shew that at the beginning the Devill G2 did talke with Eva, using the serpent for his instrument. If he could then immediately after his fall use speech, shall we doubt that be cannot now? Is it not apparátly set forth in the gospell, that Devils came out of many crying and saying, what have we to do with Jesus, and c. S. Luke Act. 19. doth shew that certain did take upon them to name over those which had uncleane spirites the name of the Lord Jesus, saying we adjure you by Jesus whom Paule preacheth, and he saith, that the evil spirite made answere and said, Jesus I know, and Paule I knowe, but who are yee? I conclude therfore out of these places of scripture, that Devils can take a bodily shape, and use speeche. -notes- G1 2. Cor.12. G2 Gen.3.

Page 31

An answere unto certaine frivolous reasons, which some doe make to prove that the Devils did not make those apparitions, and that he cannot appeare in any bodily shape. The 7. Chapter. There is nothing almost so plaine, but that there may be cavils made against it, and some probable shewe of reason, such therfore as take upon them to maintaine that Witches and conjurers doe nothing by the helpe of Devils, and that spyrites can take no visible shape, devise all the shiftes which they are able, to avoid those testimonies of scripture which I have alleaged, It is necessary therfore that ere I proceede any further, that the futility and vanity be shewed of the chief reasons which are brought for that purpose. First touching the Enchaunters of Egypt, might it not be that they made Serpents indeede by naturall Magicke, for they which do know the secretes of nature may do things straunge and mervellous, To this I answere, that if Jannes and Jambres did by there skil in the secrete power of nature, turne their staves into very serpents, I know few of the miracles of Christ, which they might not eyther doe, or as greate. Christ turned water into Wine. If those Enchaunters had bene there and by naturall Magicke had turned their staves into serpents, who would not, or might not justly have affirmed their miracle to be the greater: The workes which Christ did beare witnes of him, as he saith, to declare that he was the sonne of god. How could this testimonie bee infallible, if so greate thinges might bee wrought by the power of nature, we see then it is against pietie to bring such a thing in question, any way to beate it into mens heads. Againe, if those Magicians had such skill to worke by nature, they must needs go beyond nature her selfe, which were a foule absurdity to bee anye way graunted,

Page 32

for they could bring forth serpents at an instant, and she can not bring forth the least things that grow, or that have life but by degrees: take a little flie, first it is a sliblow, then a maggot, and afterwards cometh to have wings, both godlinesse and nature condemning such opinion of naturall magike, I will speake no further of it. It will be objected that yet notwithstanding it both not follow of necessitie that they did it by the divell, for there is a third waie by which by all likelihood it was done, If there be but a third, as indeed it is impossible to find a fourth, and that it be proved not to be by that, then it must of necessitie be left unto the first, that is to the divell. Let us see what that is: what absurditie say some can follow, if we affirme that they were very serpents indeed, and that God himself did make them, to the end that Pharaos hart might be hardened: I answer that here will greater absurditie follow, than by affirming that the sorcerers by their enchantments did make a shew of serpents, and that hee which coveteth to avoid Charibdis doth fall into Scylla, shunning one danger, lighteth into a greater, for if men will see, there is no absurditie at all to affirm that the divell did make appearance of serpents, but to saie the staves were turned into verie serpents indeed, and that God did it, doth draw a taile after it which is not sweete. If this may be, or that these two might stand together, that God doth condemne inchantments, and now worke by inchanters, yet how absurd were this for any man to affirme, that the power of God did resist and withstand himselfe, for Moses and Aaron came in the power of God, Paule saith Jannes and Jambres withstood them, if God turned their staves into Serpents, then God withstood them, and his power was opposed against himselfe, his wonders were for to fight one against another. The Lord is brought in here on both sides, I know not what other men can see, but so farre as I can judge, this is grosse impiette. Moreover, these Magicians were in great credit and estimation with Pharaoh and his princes for doing such like

Page 33

matters before him: otherwise how should it come into Pharaos minde so readely to send for them for such a purpose. Admit the king were a siely foole, and his nobles simple men, which could not espie cosenage, yet how commeth it to passe that these Sorcerers go so boldly unto the matter: Here is no place for cosenage now, there is no sleight, nor no conveiance wrought onely by man, which is able to carrie away the matter. They must now shew somewhat which is not in mans power, or else all is marred, for they shall betray themselves to be meere coseners, and so become ridiculous, and not onely that, but also the king espying their former deceits it will cost them their lives. They bee not afraid, they draw not backe, they make no excuses, shall wee imagine they did know God would turne their staves into serpents? No, we see they tooke Moses to be such an one as themselves, and therefore were bold to oppose themselves, and to withstand him, untill such time as they were even forciblie constrained to acknowledge that Moses and Aaron did worke by the power of God. This, say they, is the finger of God, whereby they secretly confesse that theirs was no such G1 power. The witch that R. Saule went onto, wrought by the divell, the thing is cleare and manifest, but there is nothing so evident, but that some shew of reason may be made against it, and that with such coullors as may deceive the dim sight of ignorant persons, this therefore must come also to be scanned, for sundry vaine and ridiculous cavils are gathered and patched together, to prove that it was neither the Devill nor Samuel, but a meere cousenage by the Witch, or by some companion, to say it was Samuel is very absurde, as we have also before shewed, and to prove that it was not the Devill, first there is brought for helpe the blind opinion of a Papist, who sayth that the Devill cannot abide the hearing of the name Jehovah which is five times named in that comunication betweene Samuel and Saull, it is to be accounted among the vile and filthy abominations of popery, that they ascribe a power -notes- G1 Exod.8.

Page 34

to drive away Devils unto words and sillabes pronounced, is every wicked man able to drive away the Devill: For there is none so vile but is able to pronounce the word Jehovah, and in deede the name Jehovah is seven times used in that place, and all by the Devill himselfe there speaking unto King Saule. I do hold most firmly that every supernatural worke is by the power of God, and to give witnesse to the truth, but heere is none, this is no miracle but such as the nature of the Devill is fit and able to accomplish. A man may wonder to see, that the same penne should write, that every supernaturall worke or myracle is of God, and is a testimonie of truth: and ye God turned the staves of Pharaos Enchaunters into Serpentes, which in very deed withstod the truth, but thus some argue the Witch did knowe Saul, add dissembled in saying that she did not, and therefore did counterfait in all the rest, to make this a necessarie consequence, there must first be proved that which is omitted, namelie that dissimulation and witchcraft are such diffentanea as cannot be found at once in one subject, or that a woman can not be both a dissembler and a Witch, proofe is made that the woman did know Saule, but with that which is weake, and with that which is false. Saul was a very tall man therefore she did know him so soone as she saw him, did she know his just stature, or was she sure there was none in all those partes so tall as the king. A wise man might sooner be deceived that way then a man of meane wit with this argument. It is saide that her house was nigh unto Saules house, which divers circumstaunces do declare, and thereby the must needes knowe him, this is utterly false, for Saul did not come unto her from his house but from the Campe. The Towne where this Witch dwelt was Endor in the tribe of Manasses. Joshua. 17. ver. 11. Saules house was at Gybeah a Cittie of the Benjamites, of which tribe he was. 1. sam. 15. 34 the Philistines had pitched their campe at Shunem in the border of Issacher. Saule had gathered the men of Israell and went and pitched nigh unto them, and from thence hee went unto the witches

house, which was not far off. The like may be said of Samuell, that he was not his neighbour, for he dwelt at Rama in mount Ephraim, whether Saule did see anie apparition or not, the words doe not flatlie affirme, but most like that hee did, though not so soone as she. If he did not see but heare a voice, can it be concluded that therefore it was cosenage, it appeareth that Saule fell downe upon his face to worship and that he which spake unto him was now in his presence. Neither is it said that the woman came out unto Saule, or that she went in unto him, but that she went unto him being fore troubled and lieng upon the ground. But the strongest reason of all is yet behind to be gathered out of the speech used unto Saule. The speech and phrase is such as agreeth not with the nature and purpose of a divell, for the papists doe confesse that the divell can not abide at the naming of God. They doe indeed, and such as beleeve them are not much wiser than they. The divell seeketh for to draw men into sinne, and not to warne and rebuke them for evill as he doth Saule. If this had beene a divell, he would have been more craftie than to leave so godly an admonition which should be prejudiciall unto his kingdome, Alacke, alacke, I see that those which take upon them to be wiser than all men, are soonest deceived by the divell. Doth not saint Paule affirme that Sathan can transforme himselfe into the likenesse of an Angell of light: Can not he or doeth not he use right excellent godly speeches mixed with bad, to the end he may deceive There can not almost be a more subtil speech to establish abhominable errors, than that which be here useth unto Saule? It is not disagreeing from his nature, nor any prejudice unto his kingdome to speake good words, to the end hee make bee hurt. Those were good words, and might seeme to be uttered unwiselie to the decay of their owne kingdome, when divels came out of many crieng and testifieing, That Jesus was the scan? of God: but they were craftilie spoken, and for a pestilent

purpose, and therefore Christ chargeth them to keepe silence. What an excellent speeche doth the Devill utter out of the G1 maide at Philippos, when she followed Paule and the other ministers of the gospel which were with him: These men, saith that Devill, be the servants of the most high God which declare unto you the way of salvation: What can be spoken more pithely in fewe wordes to set foorth the dignity of the Apostle and his companions: What can more commend the certainty and preciousness of their doctrine, he setteth foorth, and commendeth those ministers of the Gospel, to be the servants of the most high God. What saith the Apostle more by the spirite of God when he doth move men to esteeme of him not as of a common person? Is not this the greatest dignitie he challengeth, Paule a servaunt of God, an Apostle of Jesus Christ: What is more precious then salvation: Who ought to be more welcome: Then they whose doctrine doth guide men in the way thereunto: God himselfe doth send it, it must needes be infallible. Doth S. Paule say any more in effect, when he calleth the Gospel the word of reconciliation? And saith they were Embassador from God to doe the message: Did the Devill forget himselfe at this tyme's Was he desirous indeede that Paule should be had in honour, and that men should harken unto his doctrine, to learne the way of salvation? Would hee goe about to throwe downe or diminish his owne kingdome, or was he so sottish that he did not knowe what was against himselfe: This is more straunge, that the Devils which gave aunsweres being accounted Gods, and credite given unto them and worshiped as Gods among the Heathen, would yet give such a testimonie, there was no commendation esteemed so among the Heathen, such as at that time were the people of Philippos, so much as the commendation which Apollo gave of any man. For now they thought, even a God had spoken it which could not lye. This might seeme to be the way to set all in admiration of Paule. But the blessed servant of GOD, did knowe the -notes- G1 Act. 16.

craft and malice of this cursed fiend: and tooke it grievously that he should take upon him to be as a fellow minister with them, even a Preacher of the Gospell, If any man will be so bolde or rather impudent, to affirme that this was not the Devill which gave aunsweres in the word, and which utters this goodly speech, but was some cosenage, I will saye no more but this: let all men peruse the historic set downe by S. Luke, and judge indifferentlie, whether the holy spirite of truth affirming one thing be to be credited, or vaine and men maintayning the contrarie. Let us observe further some other circumstances and we shall easily see it was not the Witch nor any man or woman which spake thus unto Saul. First this is a cleare case, that the Witch could not for certaintye know that Saul should be overthrown. For to say that the people had forsaken him is utterly false, he had (as the holy ghost reporteth) gathered all Israell unto the battell, and mustered a great army, Saul was afraid, but yet hee kept it close from the people, for they set valiantly upon the boast of the Philistians, and fought with them, then if the woman could not knowe for certaintie that Saul should at that time be overthrowne, how durst she plainly tell him that he should die, and that within so short a space, even the next day? If he had escaped at that time, would it not have coste hir the best bloode in her bodye: Would not hit cousenage have bene espied, and how she had terrefied the king to his danger: no punishmet could be sharp enough for such a fact. It will be aunswered that the Devill could not know for certainty that Saul should be overthrown. It is very true, but yet he could collect more certainly then any man, he did see more on both sides then the Witch coulde gather by a few wordes, he knew what was the strength and courage of the Philistians, and that they purposed to fight the next day, and what doubt was in the hart of Saul, the woman could not be sure when the battell would be. He did know ye God would cast off Saul, as he had spoken by Samuel, the most part of the people did not regard what God spake by his servaunts

Page 38

the Prophets, so that we may well thinke (that if the poore Witch heard here what Samuel sayd) yet she could not tel when, nor in what maner, nay she was one which regarded not the voice of gods Prophets, for if she had, she would not have bene a Witch. If the devill were deceived and that the K. had escaped yet he needed not to feare, there was no waye to punish him, he durst speake boldly and reprove the king, the surest way for the Witch (if she had used but cousenage) had bin to tell Saul a smooth tale to flatter him, and to incourage him unto the battell, for then if he had fallen, he could not come againe to reprove hir, if he had escaped, He should have bene had in great estimation, end richly rewarded. And who is so simple in the knowledge of Gods word and the Histories set forth therein, but must needes confesse, that it hath alwayes bin the manner of couseners and flatterers to tell Kinges of prosperous and good successe, and to speak pleasaunt things. Wherefore do couseners and flatterers practise their lewdenesse, but for favour and gaine: Can any be fit for such a purpose, which is so foolishe as to tell a King that hee shall he destroyed: Was this Kinge Saul growne contemptible and of no power: Wee may see in the Historie that hee was of greate force and dealt cruelly. For he destroyed Nob the Citie of the Priestes with the edge of the sworde, hee persecuted David, and had many to set him on, durst now a poore woman despise him: Was the forme of words used by Samuel so commonly bruted abroad, and in everye mans mouth, that the verie Witch had it so perfectlie. Men will not speak that which is against the King and to his dishonor in the dayes that he liveth. If those wordes of Samuel were publikly spread among the people, yet they were not beleeved, but of the smallest part this is plainely proved by this, that after the death of Saul, the most of the Tribes of Israel did not admitte of David whome Samuel had anoynted, but cleave unto the house of Saul, and made ware. David was now in Bavishmente fled out of the Countrye, there was no shewe that he should be King, and yet in this

Page 39

speech unto Saull it is said expresly, God will rend the kingdome from out of thy hande, and give it to David. I doubt not but whosoever considereth these thinges, and is not wilfully bent to maintaine his owne conceite, hee will confesse that this was the Devill, who knoweth what God speaketh by his prophetes, and is right sure it will come to passe. Whereas the most part of men never regarde what the Lord hath spoken. G1 The Devill did speake unto Eva out of the Serpent. A thing manifest to proove that Devils can speake, unlesse we immagine that age hath made him forgetfull and toungue tyde. Some holde that there was no visible Serpent before Eva, but an invisible thing described after that manner, that we might be capable therof. The reasons which are brought for proofe are more then frivolous, and therefore I will but briefely touche them. It was the Devill himself and not a snake which seduced Eva, that is moste true. For who doth maintaine that the beast was any more but the outward instrument which the Devill used. This instrument was not a snake, but one of the greater beasts. For Nachash doth not onely signifie a snake, but also the beasts which is called a serpent. Whereof there be divers kindes and some greater then other. Behemoth are beasts among which worms are not reckoned, and this Serpent is matched with them, as one of them? When it is saide thou are cursed above everye beaste. It is further saide, that if heere by the name Serpent were ment both the Devill and a beast, the holy ghost would have made some distinction, that we might bee enformed, as though it were such an absurdity to set foorth the story as it did at that time appeare unto Eva, and to comprehend under the name of that which was visible and knowne being the instrument, the chiefe worker who was unknowne and invisible: Eva did not as yet know of the fall of Angels, shee knew no name of Devill or Sathan, she did not understande that there was a Devill, no doubt God did instruct both Adam and Eva that there was another besides that visible serpent, -notes- G1 Cen. 3.

Page 40

when he promised them victory by Christ, further this is objected, that the Devill is called a Serpent by an Allegorie, and therefore what necessity to take it there of a beast: I answere that the Devil indeed is by a metaphor called a serpent in many places of holy scripture. But doth it therefore follow that in this place was none but hee? The storye doth plainely evince that he covering his practise by the beaste and using him for his instrument, hath ever after the same name given unto him. And for learned interpreters of that Historie, as Maister Calvine and others, what jugling is it to allege some of their sayings contrarie unto their meanings, which do very well accorde with this, that the Devill spake out of a beast indeede. It is thought a poore Snake should not have the curse layde uppon him, for how could hee be guilty of anye sinne: This cannot stande with the justice of GOD. I aunswere that Maister Painter hath deceaved many which take it to be a Snake, and touching this beaste the serpent, it standeth with the justice of God that he should be accursed above every beast. He is an ignoraunt man that knoweth not that every beast, and the very earth it selfe had a curse laide upon them for mans sinne, they did not offend but were made for mans sake. Then if God in justice layde a curse uppon them, as to saye it were not in justice because they did not sinne were blasphemie, how should it seeme straunge that God should curse the Serpent above every beaste, who was the instrument of mans fall, though hee knewe not what hee did: But to let those goe, this is the chiefe and principall, for the matter which I have undertaken, to shewe even by the very storye that there was not onely the Devill, but also a very corporall beaste. If this question hee demaunded, did Eva knowe there was anye Devill, or anye wicked reprobate Angels. What man of knowledge will say that she did? She did not as yet knowe good and evill. She knewe not the authour of evill. When the Lorde sayde unto her, What is this which thou hast done: she answereth by and by, The serpent deceived me. Shee saw there was one which had deceived hir, shee nameth him a serpent, whence had she that name for the devill whome face had not imagined to bee? It is plaine that she speaketh of a thing which had before this received his name. It is yet more evident by that she sayth, yonder serpent, or that serpent, for she noteth him out as pointing to a thing visible: for she useth the demonstrative particle He in the Hebrew language, which severeth him from other. Anie man of a sound mind maye easilie see that Eva nameth and pointeth at a visible beast, which was nombred among the Beastes of the fielde. The curse is directed to both under one, because they were joyned in one touching the worke, some thing in it cannot belong to the Serpent, as the victory by Christ. Likewise no allegorie can well mollifie some speeches to apply them unto a spirite, as to goe upon his brest, to eate dust all the daies of his life, then we see that Devils can speake. And the Devill did speake out of aman Act. 19. for the holy ghost doth affirme it. G1 There were saith Saint Luke, certaine of the runnagate Jewes, which were exorcistes that tooke uppon them to name over those that had evill Spirites, the name of the Lorde Jesus, saying, wee adjure you by Jesus whome Paule preacheth. And they were certaine sonnes of Sceva a chiefe Prieste a Jewe, which did this thing, the evill spirite answered and said, Jesus I knowe, Paule I knowe, but who are ye? the man in whom the evill spirit was, ran upon them and did prevaile against them. We see it flatly said, the evill spirit, and not the man said, Jesus I knowe, Paule I knowe, and c. Why should we doubt then, but that devils, when God doth permit can speake: I knowe not what colour of reason can be alleged against this, unlesse some will say it was long ago: let it bee shewed that such a thing hath beene of later times. There might be, ye see, if God permit, and no doubt -notes- G1 Act. 19.

there have bene many at all times: though there have been also and are many notorious counterfeits, if devils can speake, yet there is a reason made by some, which boasteth it selfe to be unanswerable, that spirits can take no visible shape. It is G1 gathered from the worde of Christ unto Thomas, thou doest believe because thou hast seene Thomas, he saith not because thou hast felte. I aunswere that as Thomas would not trust his sight, but would have it confirmed by feeling, which was graunted him: so Christe putteth the one sense, namely the sight, for both sight and feeling, or for a sight confirmed by seeing G2 this is proved by Christs owne wordes in Luke 24. For be saith handle me and see: when they were afraid and thought it had bene a spirite, why doth he not say handle and feele: I conclude therefore that it is a thing most certaine by the word of God, that Devils can both speake, and take a visible shape upon them, when God doth permitte. No man nor woman can give power unto the devill to doe hurt, neither doth their sending authorize him, but he useth them onely for a colour. The 8. Chapter. Hitherto wee have declared in some measure the nature and power of Devils. How it resteth that wee speak somewhat touching those instrumentes whome they use for the practise of their wicked deceipt. For the uncleane spirits are the doers in sorceries and witchcraftes: men and women are but instrumentes. It is the common opinion among the blind ignorant people, that the cause and the procuring of harme by witchcraft, proceedeth from the Witch, and that either the Devill could or would doe -notes- G1 John 20. G2 Luke 24.

nothing unlesse he were sent by her. How absurd this conceite is, shall easily appeare if wee weigh these few rules. First al men that have the use but of naturall reason, must needes confesse that witchcraft and conjuration are to bee nombred among these filthy sinnes which are most abominable and odious in Gods sight, this is also as cleere, that the fowlest sinnes do spring and flow from the moste uncleane Fountaine, though men be corrupt by nature and very vile, yet the Devils are muche worse. They bee the authours and devisers of sinne, they drawe men into it, the Devill then hath devised witcherye, conjuration; and Enchauntment. The Devill allure th and seduceth men to become Witches, Conjurors, or Enchaunters, he seemeth to be a servaunt unto the Witch, but shee is his servaunt. The conjurors suppose that they bind him by the power of conjuration in which they reckon up the names of God, but he is voluntarily bound, or doth indeed but faine himselfe to be bound, for shall we thinke ye he would devise and teach an art wherby he should indeed be bound: Or can any man be so blockish as to imagine that god will in deed bind him by his power at the will of a Conjuror. Againe we may not thinke that he which is more forward unto evill and mischiefe, is set on and procured by the lesse forwarde unto evill, for that is preposterouse, then muste wee graunt that the Witch doth not provoke forward the Devill, but the Devill bearing swaye in the heart setteth hir on. Hee sayth shee sent him, but from whence commeth it that she sent him? Did be move hir for to do so? He doth harme, shall we suppose that she gave him commissió and power, let it be examined, first we confesse that god ruleth all by his providence. G1 Next this is taught us also in the holy scriptures, ye the devill ruleth with power in the children of disobedience, hee is the god of ye world, G2 sinful men are by a righteous vengance of god subject unto him, what shal we say then, can ye lesse give power unto the greater, shall a silly old creature scarce able to bite a crust in súder, give autortiy and power to ye prince of darkness: is - notes- G1 Ephef. 2. G2 2. Cor 4.

Page 44

any man so simple to beleeve that the Devill can have power given him but from a greater then himselfe: or when hee hath liberty, wil hee not execute his power unless some witch send him: what is a witch then: what is a conjurer: what is an enchaunter: surely the very vassals and bondslaves of the devil: they have no power to do, or to authorize him to do any thing. But hee being the minister and executioner of Gods vengeance, whe God giveth him power he useth them as his instrumets. not to receive helpe by them for when can they helpe him but onely for a colour, that be may draw multitudes into sinne by meanes, as indeede hee doth. This shall appeare fully in that which followeth: and therefore I will onely touch it here by the way, and stand no longer about this point which is manifest enough. That the Devill practising his mischiefe by sorcerers, doth lead the wicked world into many horrible sinnes which snare the soules of men unto eternal condemnation. The 9. Chapter. If this be maintained that ye witch is but an instruemt under a colour, then some will demaund what great thing Satan gaineth by such. I answer that be gaineth that which he endevoureth above all things to bring to passe: and that it is to lead men into the depth of sinne, that they may be drowned in the deeper condemnation. He wayeth not so much the plaguing of mens bodies, or hurting their cattle, as hee doth that. Here therefore is the chiefe matter of all, which is to disclose, and lay open the subtilty, the errors, and sinnes, which by this meanes he draweth men unto, I will first begin with the conjurer and the

Page 45

witch, and all those which use enchantment. How miserable is their case, which are so fallen from the living God, to have society and fellowship with devils: The conjurer estemeth him selfe to be a great Lord and commaunder even of devils, and in deed hath no power to do any thing further then Satan is willing and receiveth power from God, and moveth his wicked heart to deale in. This great bynder and commaunder or Devils, hath his own soule bound and commaunded by them, and is in miserable and vile captivity. The Witch is not also great, but yet the pore old hagge thinketh her selfe strong, that shee hath two or three servants as she may seme to plague such as she is offended withall. Alas what an horrible state hath the feind brought her into, who seemeth to be her servant, and yet commaundeth her, and ruleth in her heart even as her God. What greater victorie then that which be hath gotten oversuch: The charmer often times knoweth no devil: but with his charme of words he can catch rattes, and burst snakes, take away the paine of the tooth ache, with a paire of shears and a sive, find out a theife. Many other pretie knackes hee glorieth in, as if he had attayned great wisedome. The art is devilish, when any thing is done the devil worketh it, he is the instructer of the enchanter, and so indeed his Lord. What should I speake of al the rest, one word may suffice, they bee horrible deluded by the subtil serpent, and made his bondslaves. This were much, though Satan could obtayne no more but even to draw those miserable caitifs into so deepe a degree of wickednes. But this is not the chiefe thing he seeketh by meanes of these to plunge the blind world headlong in the gulfe of wicked apostasie. And how he hath prevailed were a great and long travell to set forth, only a taft may suffice. In old tyme among the heathen, and prophane nations he prevailed so farre that hee was taken to be God. Disillusions, were restrained to bee by a devine power, for so S. Luke reporteth. Act. 8. where hee sheweth that Simon Magus had long tyme by Magike astonished the Samaritans, and they sayd hee was the great power of God: untill the power of God did appear

Page 46

indeed by the woonders which Phillip wrought, for then his were disclosed to be but illusions, sleights and shewes of wonders. For though the devill can do thinges which are strange and wonderful unto man (as be did by Simon make the Samaritans woonder) yet in very deede they bee no true miracles, neither can he worke any though God should give him leave to shew all his power. Further also among the heathen his answers were taken for the very oracles of God. From hence sprong the filthy maner of woorshipping devils, abhominable idolatry, and superstitions. Therfore the Lord commaundeth his people when hee had brought them out of Egipt that they should not geve eare unto such as the heathen did. Hee promiseth for to rayse up alwayes unto them a Prophet, at whose mouth they should learne to know his will, unto whom they should harken. Deuteron. 18. We see then it is very manifest that while Satan stood in reputation to bee God. He applyed himselfe by witches and enchauters to set up a religion where hee might bee most devoutly worshipped. The most of all his practises tended to that purpose. At the comming of Christ, by the light of Christ, by the light of the Gospel, he was disclosed, and could cover himselfe no longer under so goodly a covering but was knowen indeed to be a Devil. Now he must walke as a Devil and secke to deceive after an other sort. And herein his subtilties have also excelled, to the great increase of wickednes among the people. For when the light of Gods word was suppressed, as it was in the popery, then was a way made for him, to worke all his feats. Then did conjurers and witches, and enchanters abond. Then were al manner of charmes rife and common. Then were a thousand magicall inventions and toyes. To set forth all particulers were infinite, therfore some few shall serve for all the rest. Satan hath a throne and a kingdome in the hart of every man, until such time as hee bee regenerate by the holy word of God, and that the power thereof be in him. He holdeth the hart in blindnes and infidelitie, and filleth it full of all filthy lusts of sinne. He knoweth well that if he be espied, men could not but with

Page 47

horror abhorre there miserable estate, and seeke after some remedy. Hee doth therefore secke to deale closly. Hee would make men beleeve that he is not nigh them. What redier way hath he to bring men into that opinion, then that they may suppose he is not abrod unles he be fetched up by conjurers, and breake away from them: If there be any terrible tempestes, and mighty thunders which set foorth the glory of God, then is he abroad. If hee can then get leave of God, (as the wicked world is worthy that God should give him power to deceive them) hee will shew himselfe by some likelines in the middest of the storme, or else declare his presence by rending up some trees or shewing some terror one way or other. Now there is great feare, for many beleeve that the devil is abrode indeede, and hath raysed by the windes, and brought the thunders. Then tales flie, and rumors are spred abrod, that there have bene conjurers. They be taken say some, and the matter confessed. Three devils are broken loose, and others say five: thus is Satan magnifyed, when as the great woorks of God are ascrybed unto him. He carieth away the glorie which the almighty should have. How vile a thing is this: most miserable in this behalfe was the state of popery: for the great prelates and grave fathers did beleeve this and led the people unto it. And see what devise they had. When any violent tempest came, they had the hollowed bell in every steeple to bee rung, which did repell and keepe him backe. For hee could not come within the sound of that. They had conjured water to sprinkle in every corner of their houses, they had holy bread and crosses, that be could rest no where. These were his owne inventions for to mocke the people, for he made them beleeve hee was driven away by these, when as in the meane time he ruled in their hartes. Do come now to the witch, what hurt doth thee: If yee aske the common people, you shall have this answere: shee is the very pestilence of the earth, all calamity is brought upon men by her. She killeth men and beastes. She tormenteth men, and she destroyeth mens goods. No man can be in safety so long as shee liveth. Woe hee unto him which doth displease

her, thrise happy are they which do not meddle with her. Is not this foule havocke trow yee, which the witches do make? Yea but how is it possible that poore old women should do such thinges: I say, they do it not by themselves. They have their spirites which they keepe at home in a corner, some of them two, some three, some five: these they send when they be displeased, and wil them for to plague a man in his body, or in his cattle. This matter hath bene tryed: for divers well disposed men, even for very pity to see what hurt witches do by sending their spirites, have seriously taken the matter in hande, and have hunted those puckrils out of their neastes. And what have they found? they have found that some one woman hath had three. They have found where shee kept them in wooll. What meate shee gave them. What likenes they had. What were their names. Whether they were hees or shees, and how many men they had killed. Some have bene hanged, and have at the gallowes confessed the whole matter. Who is able to declare the brutish errors and foule sinnes which multitudes are led into, by this craftye dealing of the dealing of the Devil. For my selfe I do not thinke that I can shew the tenth part. But yet I see so much as may make any Christian hart bleede to beholde. I will endevor to open the collusion of Satan and his purpose in this thing, so far as I can: with the follies which the blinde multitude fall into, and do not espie the same. First then for the maner. The poore old witch, pined with hunger, goeth abroad unto some of her neighbours, and there begged a little milke which is denied. Shee threatneth that she will be even with them. Home shee returned in great fury, cursing, and raging. Forth she calleth her spirite, and willeth him to plague such a man. Away goeth hee. Within few howres after the man is in such torment, that he can not tell what hee may doe. Hee doth thinke himselfe unhappy that he was so foolish to displease her. What shal wee say unto these things: Is here no packing: Is not here first of all a way taken by the wiely and wicked

serpent to bring men in beliefe that hee is not nigh them, nor medleth not unlesse his dame send him: Hee goeth about like a roaring Lyon, seeking whom he may devour, as Saint Peter sayth. Shall wee bee so sottish to beleeve that hee lyeth at the witches house: hee is a mighty tyrant, if God do suffer him, that hee beyng a spirite do take upon him the shape of some little vermin, as cat or weasill, it is but to deceive. He lyeth and sleepeth in warme wool, the witch doth give him milke, or a chicken, and hee doth eate, these are vain illusions, what needeth hee such thinges: he resteth not, hee eateth not, he slepeth not. How much greater folly is it to enquire of his sexe: as though there were hee deuils and shee devils? But to come nigher unto this tragedie. Doth not shee send him: yes shee doth send him which did send her first. Who put into her heart to begge of that man? had bee no stroke in the matter that shee would denie her request? are they not for the most part in as great blindnes and infidelity almost as the witch is, which are bewitched: hee knoweth well ynough where hee maketh his match. Shee doth furiously rage and curse: doth not the devil worke it in her heart: wel, the man is tormented indeede, who doth that: here is great cunning. Sometime he doth it: sometyme he maketh a shew that he doth it, when it is not so: when hee doth it who geveth him the power: did the witch: they bee voide of reason which thinke so. Had hee power and lay still while shee sent him, not minding to do any thing, unlesse hee were requested: what foole can imagine that? How is this thing then: doubtles this wicked devill either did know that God had geven him power, and so did sterre up and set on the witch: or else be did see great likelihood that God would give him leave to torment the man in his body or his goods because of his wicked life and infidelity. For hee is never wearie, but seeketh all occasions. And we have so flat testimonies of Gods word, that where God gave him leave hee tormented the bodies of men, that such as affirme hee can not plague that way, shew themselves over bold agaynst the truth. Wee see then it must needes bee one of these for this first point, hee tormenteth

the man: For God did geve him power, but hee would for many causes be set on by the witch, where she could not increase his power: or else he doth conjecture that the Lord will give him leave when he is sent, because the people are worthy to bee seduced and lead into vile errors: sometyme he seemeth to do that which hee doth not, and that is with much subtilty. For hee seeth the humours in the bodies of men, and beasts. Hee seeth the rootes and causes of diseases, and when they wil come foorth. Hee sterreth his dame, or rather his poor vassal and setteth her in quarell with that man. Shee sendeth him, the man falleth lame, or into some languishing sicknes, his hogges or his kyne do die. There was natural cause of lamenes of sicknes and death which the Lord sent, and Satan would have it layd upon him. The witch seeth such effectes follow, and gathereth for certaynty that she did it. The man calleth to mynd how hee displeased her, and how she did threaten him, and now is sure she did it. These are part of his wayes, let us looke further. He is a bloody murtherer and delighteth to draw men into perjury and cruelty. Hee seeketh therefore to bring many such unto their death for witchcraft as are no witches. Some woman doth fal out bitterly with her neighbour: there followeth some great hurt, either that God hath permitted the devil to vex him: or otherwise. There is a suspicion conceived. Within fewe yeares after shee is in some jarre with another. Hee is also plagued. This is noted of all. Great fame is spread of the matter. Mother W. is a witch. She hath bewitched goodman B. Two hogges which died strangely: or else hee is taken lame. Wel, mother W doth begin to bee very odious and terrible unto many her neighbours, dare say nothing but yet in their heartes they wish shee were hanged. Shortly after an other falleth sicke and doth pine, hee can have no stomacke unto his meate, nor hee can not sleepe. The neighbours come to visit him. Well neighbour, sayth one, do ye not suspect some naughty dealing: did yee never anger mother W?truly neighbour(sayth he) I have not liked the woman a long tyme. I can not tell how I should

Page 51

displease her, unlesse it were this other day, my wife prayed her, and so did I, that she would keepe her hennes out of my garden. Wee spake her as fayre as wee could for our lives. I thinke verely shee hath bewitched me. Every body sayth now that mother W is a witch in deede, and bath bewitched the good man E. Hee can not eate his meate. It is out of all doubt: for there were which saw a weasil runne from her houseward into his yard even a little before hee fell sicke. The sicke man dieth, and taketh it upon his death that he is bewitched: then is mother W apprehended, and sent to prison, she is arrayed and condemned, and being at the gallows, taketh it uppon her death, that shee is not gylty: and doubtles some are put to death not veyng gylty. Now let us see what the devil hath gayned by this practise. For though at sometymes the conjectures fall out right, yet many times there is innocet blood shed: which is a grevous sin. The jury commit perjury and cruel murther, which uppon blinde surmises of ignorant persons, do give their verduite, for they should see what knowledge of God, the accusers have. Yea sundry tymes the evidence of children is taken accusing their owne mothers, that they did see them give milke unto little thinges which they kept in wooll. The children comming to yeares of discretion confesse they were enticed to accuse. What vile and monstruouse impieties are here committed: It falleth out sometyme that some visitation lighteth uppon some person man or woman. Either the devill doth torment indeed, or els the party faineth to be tormented(which hath bene often seene)and then accuseth such a woman to have sent the devil. It is strange to see the madnes of the people, that wil aske the devill who sent him. And then he telleth who is his dame, and to how many she hath sent him, and how many hee hath kylled. If it were the Devill indeede, would they beleeve him: Is it not his desire to bring innocent persons into daunger? Would not hee very gladly have a number of men perjure and forsmeare themselves: doth the Lord will men to goe upon their oth in a matter, at the testimony of a devill:

Page 52

Who would thinke that ever such brutish ignorance should be found in men, in the tyme of the Gospell: This is also a practise which would make a man tremble to thinke upon it: that there should ever such abominable beastliness bee found in a land where Christianity is professed. It they doe suppose that one is bewitched, they enquire after a wise man or a wise woman, to learne who hath done the deede. If it be not meere deceipt but that the partie hath a devill, and telleth them indeed the man is bewitched, and describeth such or such an olde woman. Yet let me aske a few questions. First, I demaund whether it be allowed for any man to deale with the devill? Is not that man by the commaundment of God to be put to death which hath a familiar spirite: Are not they then almost as evill as he, which seeke unto him? No doubt it is a cleere case and cannot be coloured. But I shall after have occasion to proove it by the testimonies of the holy Scripture, and therefore I doe omit the same now. Then further I do demaund whether they will beleeve the devil: Do they thinke he will accuse a giltie person or an innocent soonest? Doe they or can they imagine that the devill will betray any thing that shall do good? Will one devill doe that which shalbe to the hinderance of another: No doubt it is a just vengaunce uppon men that have despised the light, that they bee thus given over to forsake God, and to followe after devils. I will proceede yet further to lay open the filthie vices which the people are drawne into by witchcraft, whiles indeede they bewitch themselves through infidelitie. A man is sicke, his sicknesse doth linger upon him. Some doe put into his head that he is bewitched. He is counselled to send unto a cunning woman. She saith he is forspoken indeede, she prescribeth them what to use, there must be some charme and sorcerie used. The partie findeth ease, and is a glad man, he taketh it that he hath made a good market, it was a luckie hower whe he sent to that woman. For doubtlesse he did thinke that if he had not found so speedie a remedie, the Witch would utterly have spoyled him. Now the devill is driven out of him and is gone. The wise woman with her familer was too strong for

Page 53

him, O that the hearts of men were not turned into the hearts of beasts, but that they would consider. Is Satan become a weldoer? Is hee so charitable and so pitifull that hee will releeve mens miseries: Or doth one devill cast foorth another? Doth the weaker give place unto the stronger: Is Satan devided against Satan: Some man will replye that this is a commó thing and well tried by experience, that many in great distresse have bin releeved and recovered by sending unto such wise men or wise women, when they could not tel what should els become of them, and of all that they had. Shall not men take helpe where they can find it: Why do men go unto Phisicions: Let it be graunted that men finde helpe by Witches. Yet this must needes be grauted, that as it is for the most part a plague and token of Gods displeasure, where he hath power graunted him to vexe: so is it a more heavie judgement, which the wicked world hath deserved, that he is suffered to heale. For now they cannot say that the Lord is their health and salvation, but their Phisicion is the devill. As all the workes of God are good, and unto right good end: so of necessitie all Satans workes be evill and to most devilish purpose. If he have power given him to possesse and to plague the bodie: he is not driven out, (for Satan doth not drive out Satan)but healeth the bodie, to the end he may the more fully possesse and destroy the soule. His charitie and his pitie are no better. O miserable health so recovered. O wretched men so relieved: they do imagine that the devill is driven out of them, and he hath entred in deeper. For can that which is devilish, as a charme, drive out the devil? They say it is such as doth cosist of good words. It is so much the more blasphemous and abhominable. For the name of God and the sentences of his holy word, are most shamefully abused unto sorceries, which is one speciall thing which the devil doth covet. He which seeketh helpe in sicknes at the hands of a Phisicion, doth that which is lawfull being ordeyned of God. For he hath given the nature and properties unto things, which shall serve for medicine. Shall a man therefore hold it lawfull to seeke helpe at the devill. Well, to proceede

Page 54

further. A man hath a silver cup missing, all corners are sought but yet it cannot be found: straungers there came none unto his house: needes must it be one of his own servants that hath plaied the theefe. Every man denyeth the matter, and sayth he sawe it not. Here is dubble griefe, not so much for the losse of the cup, as that a man should have a theefe in his house and not know him. And which is more, it may be that he whom he most suspecteth is least giltie: were it not good to have meanes for to trye out such a matter: He could bee content to ride xl. miles to have it tryed. He enquireth secretly where there is any cunning man of great fame. Thether he hasteth, Home he returneth and in very deede findeth the cup, and Knoweth ye theefe, though he may not betray him. What shal we thinke of this: Even that one devill hath plaied the whole play, and every part thereof: and therefore it is all alike for good. First the devill tempted the servant to steale the cup: The selfe same devill put into the mind of the maister to seeke unto a cunning man. The self same devil knoweth best where the cup lieth hid and who stale it. He therfore is ye most fit and doth give the directió. But what hath ye devil gained by this he hath gained even his desire: for God letting him loose for to tempt, here followe great sinnes. First there is theft: then seeking unto devils. But because men are blind and suppose that such a seeking is no great offence, I will shew what the Lord speaketh thereof in the holy scriptures. I will first referre men unto that which the holy Ghost saith of King Saule. 1. Cronic. 10. For there we may see that there are two sinnes metioned for which the Lord did destroy Saule. The one that he spared Agag. The other, that he enquired at Ytho. The Lord hath given an express commandement Deut. 18. that his people shall not seeke unto such. The Prophet Esay chap. 8. ver. 20. affirmeth that there is no spark of light in those which doe enquire at those which have familiar spirites. It is as much as if he should say, they have no sound knowledge of God at all in them. This is a thing to he woondred at, that in places where the Gospell hath bene many yeeres taught, there should bee men found that are ignorant of

Page 55

God. But indeede they have not reverenced, but despised the light in their hearts. The Lord doth threaten sharply Liuiti. 20. vers. 6. that person which shall seeke unto those that worke with the devill. The words bee these: The soule which shall turne it selfe unto Oboth (that is, to the Spirites of Xytho) or to the Soothsayers, to goe a whoring after them: I will set my face against that soule, and will cut him off from among his people. God saith here that such persons as seeke unto Conjurers and Witches, doe goe a whoring after devilles. The soule of man should be kept pure and chast unto God as a wife unto her only husband. They should not commit spirituall whoredom with devilles, as the Lord doth here charge those which seeke unto devilles. What a foule thing is this, that such as have made a solemne vowe in baptisme, to forsake the devill and all his workes, should now seeke unto devills for helpe: Hee that committeth adulterie in the flesh, is not to bee suffered. Then how much more are these worthie to bee rooted out, which have so unfaithfully broken their vowe made unto GOD, and have committed whoredom with devills. If there were no other hurt but this by witchcraft, you see the devill hath gained much: when many give counsell, and many do seeke unto such as have familiare spirits, and so in effect, fall from the living God. I might stay here and proceede no further to shew what doth moove the devill to do such things by Witches, as he could do as well without them: and what doth moove him to heale such as are hurt, to reveale things which are lost or stolen, and as it were to do good. But I goe a litle further, and shew great and generall mischiefes. What greater advauntage unto the devill, then to hold men from turning unto God by repentaunce: And this hee both bring to passe by Witches, All chastisements come from God, whether they be such as hee doth with his owne hand inflict: or such as hee giveth the devill point to lay uppon men. So that whether the Lord God do it with his owne hand, or by the divell, (as hee did unto Job) or whether the devill do it without a Witch or by a

Page 56

Witch, all is one in this respect, that it commeth from God, and should humble men, and bring them unto true repentance. But men looke no further the unto ye witch: they fret and rage against her: they never looke so high as unto God: they looke not to the cause why ye devil hath power over them: they seeke not to appease Gods wrath. But they fly upon ye witch: they think if she were not, they should do well enough: she is made the cause of all plagues and mischiefs: whereas in very deed she is but an Instrument which the devill useth for a colour: their owne wickedness hath provoked God to anger, and to give the devill power over them. It is their own infidelity which hath bewitched them: they should now turne unto God, and they runne after the devill: For some fall upon the Witch and beate her, or clawe her, to fetch blood: that so her spirite may have no power. These are well after, for the devill is glad to make them Witches. For when as they ascribe power unto such things to drive out devils, what are they but Witches? Some runne unto the Witch when any friend of theirs is bewitched, and threaten her, that if she doe not take home her spirite, and if that he come any more they will cause her to bee hanged. They should runne only unto God by lively faith, true repentance and hartie prayer, to have the devill remooved; and they runne unto the Witch, and ascribe unto her that which doth belong only unto God: for they thinke that she hath power to send the devill, and to take him off. Alas, is there any true faith in these men: The devill hath bewitched them, to keepe them out of the way of repentaunce, and to make them his bondslaves. Others there bee which have their Hogges distragely or some other cattell. It may be, they be so blind and so wicked, that God hath given power unto the devill to make havocke indeede. He mooveth the Witch, and she sendeth him. Their sinnes they looke not upon, but how to overcome the power of the Witch, as they imagine. And what doe they: They take a Hogge or some other beast and burne it alive. Doth this drive away the devill? Sure if it doe, it is not because it doth

Page 57

overcome him, but because he is delighted with their burnt offering which they offer unto him. What should I stand to reckon up all the devises which they have to drive away the devill, if he have begunne to hurt them, to unwitch as they call it, or to keepe him off with their charmes, or with their night spell which they have learned: What neede is there to rehearse the knackes which they have to drive away the ague, the Tooth-ach, to make the Whay Curd: to make Butter come, to make Cheese runne: They bee all very witcheries, wrought by the devill. For it is by no naturall meanes, and to tye the extraordinary power of GOD unto such things, is verye blasphemous. These bee the fruites of Poperie, which hath remooved away the light, and left the people in the dark to be deluded by the devill: which remooved away the spirituall armour wherewith the soule should bee defended and taught the people verie witcheries. Wee see then (or at the least all may easily see) that while men are thus blinded with wicked errours about witches, they are so farre from the way of repentance, that they are carried headlong into ye pits of filthy sins which do drowne men in destruction. Wee see that it is a most clere case, that God ordreth all by his good providence. The witch can do nothing, for the devill which is farre greater then she can do nothing. But the wicked world full of all contempt of God, doth deserve that the devill should have power to worke many feates, to the end they may have strang delusion, and the efficacie of error come upon them. This doth S. Paul set foorth 2. Thess. 2. For there wee may see that Satan hath libertie given him to shewe his efficacie with the power of lying Signes and woonders. If Satan could make no shew or appearance of woonders, by doing things which are beyond the reach of man to counterfait, why should it bee called a power and efficacie, and why should they be called signes and lying woonders: Our Savior him selfe, Math. 24. vers. 24. doth shew that there should arise false Christs, and false Prophets, and should give great signes and woonders. I conclude therefore, that as the righteous God

Page 58

doth permit and suffer the devill, for the wickednes of the world, to shew foorth an efficacie and power. By giving signes and woonders (ye is such things as men are not able to doo, and therefore doo account them woonders, though they be no true woonders in deed, nor wrought unto a good end, but to establish false religion) so doth he let loose the same devill, or suffer him to doo many things by Witches and Conjurers, that the despisers of the holy religion may bee seduced. There hath bene meere cosinage in most of the popish miracles: (For if they had bene done as they report, they should have bene miracles in deede, and the devill is able to doo no miracle, but to make a shew by illusion) yet were they believed by occasion of those shewes which hee made at some times. In like manner there are straunge woonders reported of Witches and Conjurers, they have bene believed, as also many counterfaite things, because he hath power at many times given unto him to torment men, and because he doth make his vain apparitions. The sharp punishment appointed in the word of God for such as worke with the devill, and the true cause of the same, and that it is no godly zeale but furious rage, wherewith the common sort are carried against witches. Chapt. 10. The Lord God did by Moses appoint and prescribe penalties for the offences, and transgressions of his holy lawes. These were not all of one kind, but according to the degree of the trespasse, was the punishmet lesse or greater. Some sinnes are more horrible then others, and doo more provoke the displeasure of God: unto such he appointed the sharpest penalty (that is to say) death without merry. Among these were such as fell into Apostasie from the law of Moses, as wee may see Hebrue. 10. vers. 28. Or such as did persuade

Page 59

others unto Apostasie, Deut. 23. vers. 5. The murtherer might not be redeemed. Numb. 35. vers. 31. The selfe same severity is required against such as worke by the devill or that dealt with familiare spirites: for it is sayd, thou shalt not suffer a Witch to live, Exod. 22. Mechashshepha by the tropesinecdoche is in this place being but one kinde, put for al that practise devilish art. For it is very vaine and frivolous to take it, that death should bee appointed, as to a murtherer with poyson. For in another place, namely Leuit. 20. vers. 27. The Lord doth take two other kindes where he appoynteth the penaltie of death. These be his words, the man or the woman in whom there shall be Ob or Jiddegnoni, shall dye the death. Out of which places we may collect the true cause of this severitie to bee in very deede the familiaritie with devils. The devils be the utter enemies of GOD, which seeke by all meanes to dishonor him and to deface his glorie. How can any then are familiaritie with them, use their helpe, or seeke unto them, but he committeth a monstrous enormitie, and such as deserveth a thousand deaths. Moreover the Witch, the Conjurer, the Enchaunter, the Sorcerer, and the rest are the cause of foule errors and much wickednesse, much horrible abusing Gods holy and sacred name, and therefore are woorthie to dye. This being the true cause why God doth abhore such, as it is manifest, we may easily see the grosse error of the blind multitude, in this behalfe. For they hold that witches should bee put to death, and not onely that, but are inflamed with a wonderfull rage and fury to have it accomplished. I call it rage and not zeale, because it is not to a right end. For if they were so zealous of it for Gods honor it were a mervelous good thing: but in deed it is not for any zeal of God ye they be so forward, but for an other consideration. Thieves and murtherers say they be put to common deaths: how much more sharp death and tormets are witches worthy to have laid upon them? But aske them why: Oh say they, the witches send their spirits and kill and lame men: they kill young infants: they kill cattle, they raise winds and tempests, they be the very plagues of men. Here

Page 60

is a false cause, for where doo we ever finde in the holy scriptures, that Witches or Conjurers have such things layd unto their charge: I have shewed the privy packing which Satan useth in this behalfe. When men are once so bewitched as to thinke, who can live in safety while witches remaine: they run with

madnesse to seeke all meanes to put them to death, and not
onely them, but all such as are suspected. They run to Conjurers
to know if they be not witches who they suspect. They examine
witches to know whether their spirites have not told them how
many witches be within certaine miles of them, and who they be.
The Lord doth not alow one witnesse being a man in a cause of
death to be sufficient: but these would alow the accusation of
one devill if he accuse xl. persons: they thinke it a mervelouse
charitable deede where there is one that hath bene suspected for
witchery, to hire or entice children to accuse them, to practise
with some subtill maide which faineth herself to be bewitched, to
get some matter of accusation. Many Jurers never weigh the
force of the evidence which is brought, but as if they had their
oth, for conjectures or likelihoodes, they are oftentimes very
forward to finde guilty, being sicke of the same disease that the
accusers be. But some man will reply and demaund why the
people should not be so earnest to seeke their death and rooting
out? why should it be reputed as a fault? they doo it of a good
minde, and to the glory of God. In deed if it could be shewed
that they do it in regard of Gods glorie it were of a good minde
and much to be commeded: but it is manifestly to be prooved
that Gods glory is not regarded. For if the people did regard Gods
glory, they would hate witchcraft, and shew their vehemency
against it, because his dishonor is much procured thereby as
when men go for help unto his enimy: but we see they hate not
that. But if a man or child be sick, they run unto a witch, they
hate not ye joyning in compact with devils, when as they runne
for help unto them: they have somewhat lost or stole: they do
by and by fly unto devils: they make account that those be good
witches and do no harme. But in very deed they be as evill as
other witches, for they have fellowship with devills

Page 61

which is the chief fault, for those damages which they ascribe
unto witches, are not in their hand to give power to the devill for
to doo: Then if they did it for love of God they would hate these
also: but we see they do not only allow them, but make of them.
God coandeth in his law that all that have familier spirits should
be put to death, and yet I say the faithles people doo make
much of them, and alow of them. Moreover there be none more
extreme haters of witches, then such as be infected with a kinde
of witchcraft them selves: for what are they but witches (if a
man looke well into ye matter) which have their night spell, and
so many charmes and devises to avoide the daungers of
witchcraft, or to unwitch: none are more furious agaynst witches
then these, and such as of all others are ye readiest to run for

help unto the devill: therefore I may boldly affirme, that it is of a mad rage, and not of a good zeale that the most are carried withall against witches: which ought to teach men wisedome, discreation and warines when they be for to deale in such matters, especially when as it doth concerne life or death. What manner of persons are fittest for the devill to make his instruments in witchcraft and sorceries, and who are subject unto his harms. Chapt. 11. When Satan at the first enterprised the ruine and destruction of man, he did not unadvisedly set up on the worke, but in great subtilty chose him a fit instrument for the purpose, even the serpent who was more subtill then any beast of the field. He is now an old serpent, and long practised, and hath increased his subtilty by much approoved experience. He doth not nowe attempt his wicked worke, but with all ye fittest waies and meanes that hee can: hee doth observe time and place, with all other circumstances: and looke of what sort soever his worke shalbe, he seeketh covenient persons as matter to work upon; he chuseth out fit instruments to worke withall when be raiseth up some heresie to destroy ye true faith, which is with subtill shew to be defended: he suggesteth not the same into the minde of a blunt

Page 62

unlearned foole which is able to say litle: but if it be possible, he espieth out a subtil minde, which is also proud, vaine glorious, and stiffe to maintain any purpose. Likewise when he will seeme by witchcraft, he doth not hope to draw a godly man well instructed in Gods word into his net and to make him a witch: for he is not subject unto his illusions, there is light in him which the darknes can not smother. What then: he seeketh for ungodly persons, which are blind, full of infidelity, and overwhelmed and drowned in dark ignorance. If there he above all these a melancholic constitution of body, his impressions print the deeper in the minde. If they be fell and given to anger, and ready to revenge, they be so much the fitter: poverty also will help in some respect. When such a person is mooved with furie, shee curleth and biddeth a vengeance light upon him with whom the is displeased: she biddeth the devill and all the devills in hell take him: the wicked spirit who inflamed her heart is ready at hand (and if he have power to hurt ý party given him of God, or see any probability that he shall have, or know any disease ready to breake forth) and in some likenes or w some voice, doth demaud what he shall doo: it may the woman doth think it very strange at the first and is afraid to heare a thing like a cat speak:but this feare in time is removed. The cojurer is one that hath a mind addicted unto curiosity and vaine estimation: he taketh him selfe by deep skill and power to rule over devils, and therefore though he appeare fierce and terrible before him; it is not amisse:nay it confirmeth him ye more. Now for convenient matter to work upon, I cofess ye the devils are instrumets which God useth not only to be executioners of vengeance upon the reprobate, and to plague ý wicked:but also to assault, to tept, to vex and to chastise his deere children:and therefore they have sometimes leave to afflict some of these in body or substance:but ye is rare: and when it is so, Gods holy servaunts doo looke up unto him, and confesse their sinnes with humble hearts, seeking favour and release at his hands, as Job did: they turne not their eyes unto witches, they cry not out upon them, as if they were the cause: you heare not these with they were rooted out, because they

feare hurt by the:but they abhor the sin, and in zeale of Gods glory, desire that due execution may be done upon them. The devil then by his witches and conjurers prevaileth not amonge these:hee doth prevaile among an other sort of men greatly:he hath power given him to plague and to vex many of them:they have no power of true and lively faith to withstand him:they bee full of all darknes and ignorance, the heavenly light and power of Gods holy word is not abiding in them:marke it who will, and he shall finde this most true, that ye greatest part of those which cry out ye they are bewitched, that run unto witches for help, that use their charms, and seeke so many waies to unwitch, are even as ignorant, as far from zeale and love of ye gospel, and as full of vices as the very witches them selves: so that ye devil doth even with as much ease seduce and lead these men into errors by witches and conjurers, finding them in ye dark, as he doth allure the poore siley old woman to be a witch, and the Idolatrous, and adulterous masse-priest to be a conjurer. Thus much may suffice to shew what persons ye devil doth make choice of to be his instruments, and what maner of persons be deceiveth and hurteth by them. The true remedy whereby men are delivered from all feare and daunger of witchcraft. Chapt. 12. Men are glad to finde a medicine that will drive away and rid them off an ague: how much gladder would they bee to finde a present remedy to preserve them safe and free from the feare off all imagined hurt and danger which cometh by witchcraft:but it is a merveilous thing to see in what feare men are and yet will not imbrace ye wholsome remedy which the Lord hath prescribed: they seeke many meanes, and that with cost and travell, but yet they are never the better: for if they finde some ease unto the body, it is with the losse of ye soule:the devill him selfe did invent those medicines which they fly unto, for God never appointed them, is he so foolish as to make weapons against

himself? if they be vexed or hanted with a spirit (as they use to say) and a witch drive him out, it is the devil ye driveth him out, if he be indeede driven out. But the trueth is, he is not:for Satan doth not drive out Satan. Put the case that one devill did expell another, what comfort could it be unto the possessed, more then this, that a weaker devill is driven out of him to give place to a stronger. For the stronger devill would never expell the weaker, unlesse it were to enter there himselfe. To let this passe, it will be demaunded where there is any remedie prescribed by the Lord against witcherie? The Lord saith he would raise up a Prophet unto the people Deut. 18. Those which give eare unto him shalbe safe. Some man will say that is but in this one poynt, that he shall not be deceived by such as wrought by the devil, nor led into error. But where is there any remedie mentioned to preserve a man from the bodily harmes done by Witches? I aunswer, that it were a straunge thing for the holy Scriptures to appoynt a medicine for such a disease as it never mentioneth. The word of the Lord doth never mention that Witches can hurt the bodie at all: and therfore it doth no where prescribe any remedie for that which is not. The malignant spirits or wicked devils, doe hurt both bodies and soules:and therefore there is a way taught how to be free from the. They have no increase of power by a Witch: but only thus much, that for the just vengeaunce of God upon the ungodly, he is glad to bee sent, and obteyneth power: but he that is armed against them alone, is armed against both witch and them. Against them there is no power ran prevaile, but the power of God. Therefore when the holy Apostle doth set men in battell against devils, he willeth them to be strong in the Lord, and in the power of his might. This mightie power of God is made ours onely by faith. For which cause S. John saith that faith is our victorie. He that beleeveth doth overcome the world: which cannot bee unless he doe overcome the prince of the world. This faith is the free gift of God: but yet because he hath ordeyned outward meanes to come unto it, we are willed to take unto us all the whole armour of God

wherein this might consisteth. And to the end that the exhortation may the more affect us, Saint Paule doth expresse the whole matter under the likenesse and termes of warre. For thereby appeareth that there is neede of Gods power, that we may escape out of the great perrill. The Apostle as a chiefe Captaine in the Lords Armie, doth stirre up and prepare all Christian souldiers. He sheweth who be the enemies. He declareth their terror in sundrie respects. But yet undoubted victorie unto all those which followe his prescript. All the power of God wherewith wee resist and overcome the devill, is conveyed into us by faith alone. But because he speaketh as of a souldier in his compleat armour, he applieth but one part unto faith, and the rest unto those things which doe goe inseparably with faith. The souldier had his head and all parts of his bodie with his legges and feete armed: then had he his sword in his right hand, and his shield in the left. Even so in this spirituall armour applyed by similitude unto the soule, here is armour for the head, for the feet and legges, and for al the whole bodie, and then the shield of faith to hold foorth in the one hand, and the spirituall sword which is the word of God in the other hand. The summe of the whole is, that by faith in the Gospell of Jesus Christ we are armed with power of grace, with true knowledge and light, with sincere integritie of heart, and with a godly life, with zeale, with patience, and with all other heavenly vertues, so that the fierie darts of the devill, neither in tempting unto filthie sinnes, nor yet in damnable heresies and opinions, can fasten upon us. If wee want the true faith, wee want grace: we be not in Christ, we have not his spirit. This faith is grounded upon the word of God: for the word is sent to bee preached, that men may heare and beleeve. If men bee ignorant in the word of God, they cannot have power to resist the devill: they have no sword to fight with him. Christ out great Captain hath left unto us an example which we ought to follow, when he resisted the devill. For at every temptation, he draweth foorth this same spirituall sworde, and saith it is written, and so woundeth Satan therewith, that he taketh the

Page 66

foyle. Moreover, as men are to bee armed with the power of GOD, so are they continually to pray for by faithfull prayer they shall obtaine a continuall supplie of grace, to overcome the new and fresh assaults of the devill. We are to give thanks also unto God at all tymes for his benefites, to depend uppon his providence, to commend unto his keeping both our soules and bodies, and all that we possesse. Thus shall the devill have no power for to hunt us: but if the Lord doe give him leave to afflict us, yet shal it be no further then may tend unto our good. For all things work together for good unto those which doe love God. Let it move us to seeke increase of faith, by often hearing of

Gods word taught: let it drive us unto continuall meditation in the same, and unto a godly life. G1 For all those which despise the glorious Gospell of Christ, or the publishing of the same, and most especially such as fight against it, doe to their power set up the kingdome of the devill, and bring in all witcherie. The light of the Gospell doth beat him downe: and therefore when Christ sent forth his Disciples at the first to preach, and they returning rejoyced, that even the devills were made subject unto them: he saith, I saw Satan fall downe from heaven like lightning. The Lord send abroad the light of his truth to throw downe Satan, and to drive away darknes from the mindes of the people. Amen. FINIS. -notes- G1 Rom. 3

www.ingramcontent.com/pod-product-compliance
Lightning Source LLC
Chambersburg PA
CBHW022041080426
42733CB00007B/923